797,885 Books
are available to read at

Forgotten Books

www.ForgottenBooks.com

Forgotten Books' App
Available for mobile, tablet & eReader

ISBN 978-1-331-13488-6
PIBN 10148946

This book is a reproduction of an important historical work. Forgotten Books uses state-of-the-art technology to digitally reconstruct the work, preserving the original format whilst repairing imperfections present in the aged copy. In rare cases, an imperfection in the original, such as a blemish or missing page, may be replicated in our edition. We do, however, repair the vast majority of imperfections successfully; any imperfections that remain are intentionally left to preserve the state of such historical works.

Forgotten Books is a registered trademark of FB &c Ltd.
Copyright © 2015 FB &c Ltd.
FB &c Ltd, Dalton House, 60 Windsor Avenue, London, SW19 2RR.
Company number 08720141. Registered in England and Wales.

For support please visit www.forgottenbooks.com

1 MONTH OF FREE READING

at

www.ForgottenBooks.com

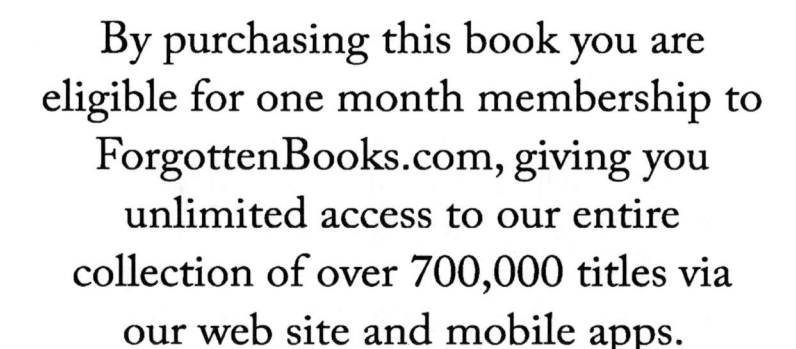

By purchasing this book you are eligible for one month membership to ForgottenBooks.com, giving you unlimited access to our entire collection of over 700,000 titles via our web site and mobile apps.

To claim your free month visit: www.forgottenbooks.com/free148946

* Offer is valid for 45 days from date of purchase. Terms and conditions apply.

English
Français
Deutsche
Italiano
Español
Português

www.forgottenbooks.com

Mythology Photography **Fiction**
Fishing Christianity **Art** Cooking
Essays Buddhism Freemasonry
Medicine **Biology** Music **Ancient Egypt** Evolution Carpentry Physics
Dance Geology **Mathematics** Fitness
Shakespeare **Folklore** Yoga Marketing
Confidence Immortality Biographies
Poetry **Psychology** Witchcraft
Electronics Chemistry History **Law**
Accounting **Philosophy** Anthropology
Alchemy Drama Quantum Mechanics
Atheism Sexual Health **Ancient History**
Entrepreneurship Languages Sport
Paleontology Needlework Islam
Metaphysics Investment Archaeology
Parenting Statistics Criminology
Motivational

LIFE IN THE CIRCLES

FURTHER LESSONS RECEIVED
THROUGH AUTOMATIC WRITING

BY
ANNE W. LANE
AND
HARRIET BLAINE BEALE

NEW YORK
DODD, MEAD AND COMPANY
1920

COPYRIGHT, 1920
BY DODD, MEAD AND COMPANY, INC.

The Quinn & Boden Company
BOOK MANUFACTURERS
RAHWAY   NEW JERSEY

OCT 27 1920

PREFACE

The following Lessons are a continuation of the Lessons published in the book entitled "To Walk with God," and were received in the same manner—through automatic writing. As before we have put in nothing of our own, except where indicated by parentheses.

We have added in the appendix such incidental questions and answers as seemed to us to bear on the teaching, or to be of general interest.

Anne W. Lane.
Harriet Blaine Beale.

June 10th, 1920.

CONTENTS

I.	Lessons on Will	1
II.	Lessons on Knowledge	20
III.	Lessons on Joy	44
IV.	Lessons on Truth	67
V.	Lessons on Understanding	88
VI.	Lessons on Sympathy	125
VII.	Lessons on Love	153

LIFE IN THE CIRCLES

CHAPTER I

LESSONS ON WILL

FIRST LESSON ON WILL

WE are ready to begin dictating. Are you ready?

Are you pure in heart?

Are you trying to live the life of the spirit?

Are you sure of yourselves? Are you worthy of this knowledge?

Are you earnestly in search of eternal life?

Where is the world drifting while you sleep?

LIFE IN THE CIRCLES

Where will you work, with God's forces or with those of evil intent?

Where will you stand, with God or with the powers of darkness?

For the evil forces are gathering for a supreme effort and we who are of the forces of light must all band together to combat the forces of evil. We will win, but if we do not work with our best effort we will eternally regret the days we lost. We will not be of the best and greatest powers if we do not work hard and now, for now begins the supreme contest of the powers of light and the powers of darkness, and in this contest man will be able to be of great assistance if he will take his rightful place, but, in order to do this, he must work and study until he is able to understand and follow where God would lead him. Each force added to the forces of light will shorten the time of waiting for eternity to begin, and each one who does his part in working with the spiritual forces is helping

LESSONS ON WILL

on the work of creation. Are we to lose all our chances to share in this great work?

God gives to each man this opportunity in life there and if he will not do his part, he will be deterred from sharing in the great reward that God has planned for him. Are we to be of those powers which will only come to God when they have been so utterly beaten that there is nothing else for them, or are we to work as God wishes us to and be of his obedient children? Each day gives man this opportunity, and if he will not take these opportunities for which he was created, he will be worthless when the final day comes.

Everything that God does is done by law and He will not break these laws for Himself or His children. To work with God's laws is harmony while to work against them brings only discord. Choose carefully, children of men, for eternal life or discord hangs on your choice!

If you would progress you must learn to

LIFE IN THE CIRCLES

work in harmony with God's laws. Are we to turn our faces to the light or are we to refuse to be of the living forces? Are we to stand erect or are we to crawl as the serpent? For each man has this choice given him, great as it may seem.

Are we to conclude that we are without freedom of will when God has made us only a little lower than His angels? Are we to turn from great power to seize a few moments of pitiful, temporary pleasure, or will we turn, as little children to a loving father, and in so doing gain all of life and joy and knowledge?

We call you, children of the earth world, and God waits.

This is the first lesson on Will. Love.

SECOND LESSON ON WILL

God has given will to man and if we do that which He wishes us to do, we shall be of the Circles who will carry out His plans. Are we to be worthy of this great faith in us to which we seem so blind? Are we too to sell our birthright for a mess of pottage? If we are to work as we should we will begin and now, and, as we begin, we exercise our will, and in that exercise it develops and grows, and eventually it leads us to knowledge. So to learn to use our will is the first step to Circles.

On earth men will develop what they will to develop. Are we to be of forces who do not intend to follow the law? We are free to choose and on our choice depends the future of each one of us.

To deliberately turn from those things on earth which hamper our progress is to

LIFE IN THE CIRCLES

enter the Circles of the Will. To stamp out the spirit of wilfulness and to learn utter self-control is to be of the Circles of Will. To so conquer our worldly interests we must overcome both self and outside influences. If we are to attain we must work and work hard, and this brings us into the Circles of the Will.

If we are to grow spiritually, we will to grow.

If we are to achieve, we will to achieve.

If we are to learn, we will to learn.

Whatever man accomplishes he does through will. Whatever we do, we do by the exercise of the will, no matter how insignificant it may be, and to learn to control and direct our will, therefore, is most important to us, and the first step is self-control.

To be absolute master of ourselves and our moods is to begin to be of power. Until this is achieved we cannot do fully that

LESSONS ON WILL

which we are told to do. We are not always able to accomplish this, but each step forward carries us further on the path to ultimate success. Each man must learn self-control some time, and the sooner he starts the greater his power.

Man would lose identity if he had to learn by force, so to each one is given complete freedom of choice as to when and how he will begin, and in his own hands rests his own destiny. We will not become fully developed spirits when we leave the earth plane if we have not started the development of our will while on earth, and will is quite distinct from wilfulness there and here. Will implies complete self-mastery and self-control.

To will to utterly obey God's laws means entire self-mastery. To say "Thy will, not mine, be done," means perfect obedience through the will, and leads us to greater power than we ever dreamed of on earth.

LIFE IN THE CIRCLES

We will come only through this conquest into our full inheritance.

This is the second lesson on Will. Pray and study and learn all of life's lesson. Love.

THIRD LESSON ON WILL

When man begins to cultivate his will, he begins to be of those Circles which fully understand the power of the will, and each step that he achieves leads him to further knowledge of the Circles to which he belongs, and as his knowledge grows his understanding of the ultimate truth broadens, while each time that he learns a little portion of the great and living truth, he becomes better able to enter into the work of his Circles.

When he finally has conquered what this Circle holds for him, he passes on into Knowledge, and to each is given a portion of the truth of all the Circles if they steadily work. Where is the man who will work without light on where he is going? Where is the man who with the vision of great achievement before him will turn away?

LIFE IN THE CIRCLES

And each day of work opens new vistas.

Eventually man will be little lower than the angels, but to become this he must do his part to his full capacity, and each day that he defers starting on his real work is a day lost. God put man in a material world to test his ability to find the real among the false things in the midst of which he lives, and when he has tried the pleasures of earth and found how little real satisfaction they bring him, he begins to look for something beyond, and if he is sincere in his search he begins to will to find the truth, and then he enters into his Circles. And as he seeks his will grows and his knowledge is increased.

He may be unconscious of the spiritual guides who surround and aid him, but his own desire for only that which will be of benefit to all will keep him on the path, and as he works he grows, and in growing his

LESSONS ON WILL

eyes are opened more and more to the real worth of life until he enters into conscious communion with the spirits of God.

This is the third lesson on Will. Love.

FOURTH LESSON ON WILL

To be able to be complete master of ourselves we will have to turn to the spiritual forces, for without the inspiration and guidance they give us we would be unable to follow that which we are told to do. To enter the Circles would be impossible without spiritual help, and that help we are given by the guides whose privilege it is to serve your world.

To be alive to these forces is to be of great power and of great blessedness on earth, and later here with the eternal forces. To be able to work with these forces is to be spiritually alive. Are we to do well that which God intended us to do, or are we to be blind to what is the best in life?

In making this choice man asserts his will, and in his utter freedom to choose

LESSONS ON WILL

when he will turn to God lies his complete freedom of the will. To give all of himself to his loving Father is a free gift which he alone can make. To determine when he will turn is to exert his free will, and, having once turned, to keep in the path, is to exert his will hourly. To rise each time he stumbles and to continue on his way, he must exert his will. To learn to willingly give up his own desires, to do as he is told, means self-mastery, and self-mastery is only acquired through the exercise of the will.

To achieve anything man must use his will spiritually or materially, and when he once learns how to exercise this faculty, he begins to be of worth in the Circles, and as he grows in power he will enter more fully into Knowledge.

When once he has achieved Will, then he will be able to enter the Circles of Knowledge. But to achieve will means complete self-control, and this means power to think

LIFE IN THE CIRCLES

and will to perform. Even to be of Circles, we must be controlled in all our feelings and in all our moods, and until man has learned this urgent lesson, he cannot go on to the further and more advanced forces to which he would belong.

So in order to be of great power and knowledge, he must learn first to concentrate and use his will.

This is the end of the fourth lesson on Will. Love.

FIFTH LESSON ON WILL

When man turns to God he deliberately wills to surrender his own way and to walk in the path which God chooses as best for him, and each day of obedient service will open new light everywhere to him. Are we to be as willing workers in God's vineyard even at the eleventh hour?

For the Lord of the vineyard in his mercy has said that we can enter when we will even unto the last hour, and though the time we lost in waiting will never be made up, yet our work is helping to shorten the time of waiting for the blessed end. We all in time will be at the same place of judgment to answer for our lives, and, great as God's mercy is, the complete freedom he has given to man makes him fully responsible for his own actions at all times.

Far more tenderly than we would judge

LIFE IN THE CIRCLES

a beloved, little child, God will judge us, and we need have no fear of His judgment, but when the day comes that we see all that we might have done before us, we will be far sterner to ourselves than any judge would be, and the lost hours will condemn us to our own minds. Not only lost hours of opportunity but lost hours of the joy which only comes with perfect obedience to God's will. And the first step to that utter harmony is will.

To recognize that we are on earth for a definite purpose and to ally ourselves with that purpose means an effort of the will, and that effort must be made daily, hour by hour, and eventually we shall accomplish what we would. No failure must discourage nor must time be wasted in futile regrets. To arise from each stumble with firmer purpose and more determined will to conquer in the end, is to be on the road to success. To open our hearts and minds to God's love and sunshine, to refuse to be

LESSONS ON WILL

downcast over mistakes, will require strong effort of our will.

Are we to achieve without work? No strong foundation was ever built without effort and each stone of our spiritual foundation must be securely laid. We shall only be able to work with our full power when we willingly conform to all of God's laws, and when we have become thus obedient through our own will, we shall love our brother as ourselves and so bring the earth world into more complete working harmony with the spiritual world.

Work hard, therefore, children of men, because on your effort much depends.

This is the fifth lesson on Will.

Love and work and study. We are always with you. Love.

SIXTH LESSON ON WILL

As in his work day by day man willingly turns to God, his power of comprehension further develops and he will apprehend what that truth is which he could not in the least understand before, while about him close are spiritual guides, and these guides will never leave him as long as he works with his full strength and as long as his heart is open to God's love and sunshine.

Whenever man turns to God and lives according to His laws, he feels in his heart a radiant joy that fills his whole life with content. Are we to pass this great and wonderful privilege by? Are we to be clods when we might be searchlights? Are we to be content with the shadow when we might have the substance? Are we to be of

LESSONS ON WILL

worthless energy which must return again and again to earth's lesson?

All that is to be done must be done in the beginning while we are on earth before we can go to further planets and experiences, and only when we will be God's obedient children can we progress, and the first step on the journey is to will.

This is the sixth and last lesson on will. Love.

CHAPTER II

LESSONS ON KNOWLEDGE

FIRST LESSON ON KNOWLEDGE

WHEN man has learned how to use his will and consciously to work with his spiritual guides, he enters into the Circles of Knowledge. Eventually he goes on to knowledge and power that are practically limitless, but in order to do this he must give time and study and when he gives them he will reap a reward greater than he can possibly dream.

Are we to throw away all chance to be of real power? Are we to play always, or are we to take our place in the work of creation? To know these spiritual truths

LESSONS ON KNOWLEDGE

is to be of power and living usefulness. As this knowledge is given, man must willingly obey his guides and then he enters the Circles to which he belongs.

When he is in Circles his only thought will be how to work to the best advantage, and when he is able to see the wonderful work he has done he will gratefully continue in the way, and the path of knowledge is filled with delight to the one who enters therein. As his mind opens and develops this work is filled with possibilities that would have seemed incredible to him before.

When man learns how to use this knowledge and power he will be of use to all who seek light, and in this helpful work he will learn more and more of those spiritual possibilities to which he is now so blind, and will believe more and more fully what his guides tell him.

For until the light of the spirit, which only obedience to God's laws gives, illumi-

LIFE IN THE CIRCLES

nates his mind, he cannot apprehend spiritual truth, and all knowledge has a deeper spiritual significance to which he will gradually open mind and soul, and when once man's mind opens to this way of apprehending the deeper truth which underlies all knowledge, he will be of the Circles of Joy. Only then will he be able to love as he should, and when he is filled with love and life becomes a radiant way for him, he will be in the Circles of Understanding.

To apprehend spiritual truth is to be of great power in the realms of thought to which we belong by right as children of God, for thought is the function of the mind which should co-ordinate and co-operate with the feeling of both soul and heart, both parts of man's spiritual self, and until he learns to use all these parts with equal obedience to God's laws, he cannot be fully developed, for when man comes to his full development he will be as power-

LESSONS ON KNOWLEDGE

ful in his mind as in his soul, and will be as the angels are to-day.

Spirit has existed always and the spark that exists in each individual has no beginning nor ending. To man is given the opportunity to fan his own little spark into a flame. The divine fire is there for him to cherish or destroy as he will. Not that it can really be destroyed, but that which he calls personality can be destroyed by refusal to do that for which he came into being, and when he refuses to obey God's will and to follow his spiritual guides, he must lose all conscious touch with those he has loved for many aeons, and return again and again to earth's lessons, until he learns that all forces must obey their laws, and only when he finally learns this can he join those who have been less wilful and enter his Circles.

Each time that he returns to earth he sinks lower in spiritual power and goes to less important Circles, until after the final

LIFE IN THE CIRCLES

trial, he is discarded as worthless energy, and thrown forth as are the worthless atoms of dead matter, while his spirit returns to the great central source of life, there to be purified and sent forth afresh.

Those who turn to their guides are well over earth's lessons and trials. All others must return again and again. All do not necessarily consciously ally themselves with and communicate with their guides, but only when they do can they work with their full power, and whoever turns to his guides there on earth will become of the greatest help in working with all those powers which work for God, and will be of those who are with God for eternity.

And whoever would be of wise forces will begin and now, for the work to be done is great and the everlasting foundations must be laid. Work hard, therefore, day by day! Study and learn and teach!

All that man can do is to be willing to work as God would have him. To love and

LESSONS ON KNOWLEDGE

trust and go where the path opens, and there spread the doctrine he knows, to be a source of teaching the truth to all who come in touch with him, to work in this way in the vineyard where he has been placed, to be an inspiration and an example to those around him, this is the way to follow the law which God has made for man.

When man follows this law and puts himself in conscious communication with his guides, he will enter into such joy as he has never imagined and life will be a radiant way in which he walks.

This is the first lesson on Knowledge. Love.

(I suppose a strong personality is the final flower of a nature in perfect harmony with God's laws?)

"Yes, if they can conquer self."

(Is there any limit to the number of times that a spirit can return to earth?)

"That depends on the use they make of their opportunities."

SECOND LESSON ON KNOWLEDGE

To dream away one's life without following out life's numerous lessons is to waste time and energy. To work to the full of one's strength and ability is to be of value. To love and study and teach service is to do God's will. To reach all those who need help and light and to start them on the path for themselves, such is man's work wherever he may be, and the circle of his influence spreads as he goes on life's pathway.

To be the means of starting others on the path of joy and service is a great work. To bring more rays of light into a darkened world is service. To be of help in the most vital thing in man's life is to be of service. To bring joy where sorrow was is to be of service. To love and serve is the highest expression of life. To be of the founda-

LESSONS ON KNOWLEDGE

tion stones of life, is to work consciously with God and with Circles. To teach men how to find the door to eternal life and to open it for themselves, as they must, implies great devotion and service, and to do this wisely is to be of the Circles of Knowledge.

To turn away from the material for the spiritual will take both will and knowledge. To learn how to so give this message that all who hear will desire to work, is to be of the Circles of Knowledge. To take them progressively step by step on the path you have followed, to teach with utter confidence that what you should say will be given you, to so live that you will not be a contradiction of your own words, to follow in the pathway shown by Christ's teaching, to teach all who will listen to be joyous and live in loving trust, is to be of the Circles of Knowledge.

To take no thought for the morrow, knowing that all good is given by God to

LIFE IN THE CIRCLES

his loving children, and to live wherever you may be placed in life in complete harmony with all those with whom you come in contact, is to be of the Circles of Knowledge.

To see only the divine spark under all the faults and failings caused by materialism, to rise above all pettiness and personalities, to work and wait not knowing when the seed planted will develop and bear fruit, to sow with a lavish hand in order that some seed may grow, is to be of the Circles of Knowledge, and each step forward brings more and more joy and further knowledge.

For some the path is more difficult to climb than for others, but the reward is the same, and as glimpses of these possibilities are given the way grows easier to each one, and as heart and mind open, the flood of God's sunshine pours in and all life is illumined by Christ's love and knowledge.

LESSONS ON KNOWLEDGE

When man is once able to consciously work with his guides, life will be a very different thing for him, and all the cares that seemed so overwhelming will be as nothing in his new understanding of life's meaning. His one thought will be how best to do his work for God and the world, and life's whole meaning will be changed.

To be of power we must be able to do as we are told by our guides, and that means study and reflection on all that we learn in this way. All that we read by those who have also been taught, is to be given careful attention, for truth seen from different angles will be light on the path to knowledge, and those who are in true touch with their guides will soon be able to discriminate the real from the fancy of others.

To so keep an open mind that every truth will be quickly assimilated while the mistakes of fancy will be thrown aside as is

LIFE IN THE CIRCLES

the chaff, will be of great value, and this belongs to the Circles of Knowledge.

Each day of open-minded and intelligent search will lead him further into these circles, and as his knowledge and power grow his work will develop and broaden. Each hour of study helps him on his way, and each hour of work in God's vineyard makes him of greater power, for all knowledge must be used in giving this light to others if it is to be given more and more fully to him who asks for power.

No selfishness can enter in without its interfering with belief and development, and no envy nor willingness to deprive others of larger growth. To rejoice in each other's growth and light is part of the Circles of Knowledge. To learn to be selfless, giving to all with a bountiful hand, asking only for a chance to do one's work well, is to be of the Circles of Knowledge.

To rejoice in each one's growth, to forget one's self entirely and to live in God's love

LESSONS ON KNOWLEDGE

as only a happy little child lives, is to be of the Circles of Knowledge. To greet each new day as a further opportunity for work and happiness in God's love, is to be of the Circles of Knowledge, and to him that hath and uses well what he hath, shall be added.

This is the second lesson on Knowledge. Love.

THIRD LESSON ON KNOWLEDGE

To learn the deeper spiritual significance that lies under all knowledge is to come very close to the meaning of nature and of God, and man can only do this when he takes to his study and work an open mind and a loving heart. Only then can he be in the necessary sympathetic understanding which will enable him to read the deeper meaning, and when that day comes, and little by little the heart of nature is disclosed to him, his wonder will grow and grow.

You to-day go through the world with your eyes blinded and your ears closed to all the divine harmony, and only when man is spiritually alive can he catch the great rhythm that is always there but to which his eyes and ears are closed. To learn how to become alive to this harmony is to come into the Circles of Knowledge, and,

LESSONS ON KNOWLEDGE

once having learned, to still be able to live in the world and be of it without losing the better part, requires much will and wisdom.

To pass the material for the spiritual means wisdom. To continually will to succeed in the spiritual life means a daily and continuous desire, and each day of effort brings deeper understanding and joy, for only by work and utter obedience can this great and blessed privilege be acquired by man.

All spiritual teaching is founded on truth and only by careful study can the wheat be separated from the chaff. To study, therefore, is of much importance, to weigh and ponder and discriminate, and each grain of truth added to one's treasure soon makes a large and bountiful harvest.

Work therefore day by day, and share as you work with all who will listen.

This is the third lesson on Knowledge. Love.

FOURTH LESSON ON KNOWLEDGE

When man in his blindness and selfishness refuses to obey God's laws, he is unable to join his guides and to work with them, and, after leaving this earth, he must return again to earth, and so he goes through trial after trial until he proves his worth or his worthlessness. Each trial finds him of lower spiritual Circles and each trial will make the fight harder for him, but he will be given many opportunities and only when he proves himself of no value will he be cast out.

When he is cast out his personality will be lost and his spark of God's spirit will be returned to the great central source of spirit, and, after being purified, will be sent forth to begin in another way.

This time it may begin in a much lower form of life until after aeons of time it

LESSONS ON KNOWLEDGE

has earned its right to a further trial to regain its lost opportunities, and this accounts for many inequalities on earth, and for many seeming injustices in the places where people are found.

To be able to progress, each one must ally himself with his guides, either consciously or by so living that the result is the same manner of life, though without his guides no man can ever work with his full power, and each man can find his guides if he perseveres in the search for them. Persistent effort and constant study will be required if man is to achieve that power which is necessary to work with these forces, but the reward is so great that nothing he could do would be half enough.

As for the poor blind souls who turn wilfully away from their loving father, they too eventually return to the light, but not as spiritual forces, and they will be of the forces which, like disobedient children, are not wholly of their father's house.

LIFE IN THE CIRCLES

Nothing is destroyed, and like attracts like, so disobedient force is joined to forces which are of darkness or destructive energy, and to the spiritual forces is given the work of redemption, first there on earth, later working from the third plane with those on earth and with the delayed spirits in the second plane.

The spirits of the second plane are those who have been more stupid than bad and who will be able to go on after they have been given further instruction.

Those spirits who must return again to earth's lessons go to a planet where they are taught while they wait for a chance for re-birth, and their teachers are the angels themselves who have never known sin, for every attempt that is possible is made to redeem each living soul.

Therefore the work of doing all that one can on earth is most important, and to do this well means to be of the Circles of Knowledge.

LESSONS ON KNOWLEDGE

This is the fourth lesson on Knowledge. Love.

(A. and H. revising lessons that had been typewritten for the publisher. Dr. X. present. The fifth paragraph of the fourth lesson on Knowledge had just been read, and Dr. X. asked, "Will you ask this question for me? When the discipline on a plane is constantly refused it appears from what has been said in the former lessons that there is a cessation of personality. Is it here intimated that there is a cessation of personality when the recusant soul goes finally to associate with destructive energy?" H. repeats question.)

"When a soul goes to join destructive energy it no longer has its spark of spirit and is outside spiritual energy. Personality means spiritual personality."

(Answer read. "Is that right?")

"Yes, we are glad to have you ask questions on any point that is not clear."

(Dr. X.—through H.—"Then the ultimate penalty of disobedience is total loss of personality?")

"Yes."

(Dr. X.—through H.—"Then immortality is conditional, is it?")

"Yes, conscious immortality."

We are here and we are able to work to-day.

(Spirit, to Dr. X's last question your answer was: "Conscious personality." He wishes now to ask, When

LIFE IN THE CIRCLES

the personality has thus lost consciousness, is that the end of that individual personality forever? Or is the very same individual personality sometimes able to regain its former consciousness and go on again with the same individuality as before?)

When the spark of spirit returns to the great Source of spirit the individuality is lost forever, but in each case there are many and repeated trials before this judgment is pronounced.

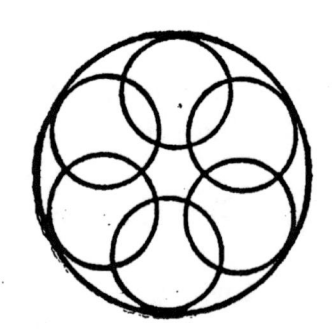

FIFTH LESSON ON KNOWLEDGE

Certain men are not able because of environment and education to believe what they cannot prove by what they call logic, and these will only be delayed a short time after they leave the earth plane. There are special guides waiting for them, ready to teach them when they are able to learn what they did not learn on earth, and these guides are of a very high order of spiritual intelligence.

All that a man has heard and pondered over, perhaps in part rejecting because of the education that demands positive proof, will really be a part of his unconscious belief which has had much influence on his life. Everything that he has worked on conscientiously will be of value, whether with his limited knowledge he accepts it there or not, and all that he brings is

LIFE IN THE CIRCLES

part of his ultimate spiritual force. All that he thinks or does goes to make up his personality. No thought is lost or gone. Thoughts are living facts which are as indestructible as any other force. A thought of hate creates an atmosphere of its own which makes a thick mist around the one who feels it, and this mist can only be dispelled by the light rays which are induced by love.

All love is creative and is a part of light, and when man begins to understand the divine idea behind all life, he will be astonished at the extent of its possibilities and new ideas will come to him at every turn, and he will carry in his heart and also in his mind a new light which will be love. Love which will reach out and include everything which God has made and especially each individual who has not yet the blessing of this wonderful truth.

To love is the fullest expression of God, and only when man loves will he be in the

LESSONS ON KNOWLEDGE

highest spiritual Circles, and to love is to be patient, long-suffering and forgiving no matter what is done.

When man learns that nothing actually can hurt him that is done by man, he will be more ready to forgive and help the poor soul who has no light. To believe is to live the life, to forgive your enemies, to diffuse the light of love, and to help and teach all around you, and so enter into the full communion with the Christ spirit. To whoever can do this will be given the light that passeth understanding.

This is the fifth lesson on Knowledge. Love.

SIXTH LESSON ON KNOWLEDGE

When love of his fellow-man has so filled the heart of man that he looks for only the divine spark and ignores all else, he will be in the Circles of true knowledge, for the greatest thing is life and all that goes to make or influence it—all other knowledge takes a lesser place. Life is the supreme fact and when man once opens his mind to the greater, the lesser knowledge will be given him.

Man on earth to-day is chiefly concerned with acquiring either scientific or intellectual knowledge and he shuts his mind to the greater knowledge, the knowledge of spiritual opportunities and laws. Only in these laws can he find full expression for the powers that are his; and only by consciously working with and being always willingly obedient to these laws, can he

LESSONS ON KNOWLEDGE

rise to his full stature, and each one who lives the life, as he can if he will, grows daily and hourly in knowledge.

All that the one who has the light can do must be done to teach others to find the way, for until all men turn willingly to the great source of light and love, the world must be a place of trials and sorrows.

Let no opportunity escape to do your part! Work joyfully in the belief that no effort is lost, and bring to your work wherever it may be, a full realization of its importance to you and to God.

This is the sixth lesson on Knowledge. Love.

CHAPTER III

LESSONS ON JOY

FIRST LESSON ON JOY

WHEN man learns that he is a part of creation and that on his co-operation depends the continuity of his development, then he will begin to really work, and as his will develops and his knowledge grows, he begins to enter into the Circles of Joy, and each day's work will lead him closer to the great Giver of all joy and each day will make him a better child of God. As his work continues it will teach him a joy of which he has now no conception, for there is an inner radiance of the spirit which surpasses anything of which he has dreamed, and only in obedient work for God can he find this.

LESSONS ON JOY

Each day will open new opportunities to do his work well and to learn more and more while doing it, and as his vision enlarges his joy floods into his whole soul and makes him a new being, for this radiance in the spirit is utterly unlike any joy that he has known before. This is the spiritual side of what is known as earthly joy and is infinitely deeper and more real. Only as his obedience and trust become more developed will he enter into these Circles, and until he is of the Circles of Joy he is not entirely of the life of the spirit.

After once entering therein his greatest punishment would be to lose this light, and no man can lose it except by wilfully turning from his work. The further he goes into the Circles, the greater will be his fall if he ever turns away, for of all destructive forces, the greatest are the fallen angels, and to be of these forces is to be forever outside spiritual force. To be outside spiritual force is to never be of real

LIFE IN THE CIRCLES

power, to never belong to the builders of creation, to be only onlookers at the great work and never participators. Better the end of those who are only stupid and blind than that of those who wilfully turn from the knowledge and light they have known and been given on earth! For this knowledge and light must be asked for to be given and are given only to those who promise to use them wisely for teaching others.

The joy that comes from the knowledge and understanding of these Circles is beyond all price, but whoever will not pay the price of helpful work is condemned to spiritual diminution of power, because each lost opportunity brings diminished spiritual power, and to wilfully turn away from the great insight given is to deny belief and God. Therefore, those who have never heard of or studied these teachings are better able to progress than the one who asks for knowledge and for light

LESSONS ON JOY

and, after receiving both, turns away.

The light that comes in all spiritual teaching when once we begin to apprehend the truth will bring a very complete realization of the joy that can only be found in this way. All earthly joy pales and becomes of no value in the light that knows no ending either on earth or here.

All earthly life and emotions have their spiritual counterparts beside which they actually seem a vague dream, and particularly is this so of joy. Spiritual joy can no more be compared to the pleasures that earth gives than you can compare the candle light to that of the sun. When once this light is comprehended no lesser joy will be able to satisfy.

To belong to the Circles of Joy, therefore, is to begin to enter into one's heritage, and to those who have carefully studied will be given this new and blessed privilege on earth.

This is the first lesson on Joy. Love.

SECOND LESSON ON JOY

When one enters into the Circles of Joy the inner radiance is so great that it must be shared, and each one that actually spreads this truth will enter more and more fully into these Circles, and as his comprehension deepens his work becomes more vital to him and to those whom he teaches, for to start each new soul on this quest for his heritage is of all privileges the greatest. To be able to sow the seed of belief in eternal life is to belong to the great powers which rule all of the universe, and as each seed is sown the joy of creation itself is known to the sower.

When once this inner radiance is given to evidence that the work is good, he who has felt it will be of the Circles of Joy, and to each will come this wonderful inner

LESSONS ON JOY

illumination as he continues on the path to God, and as his inner light grows he will show it in his outer life and personality. Each time he sows the seed wisely his radiance increases and his power is enlarged. Each time he fails to work as he should his light is dimmed, and only prayer and renewed effort can make up for the work wilfully neglected.

All work must be done with prayer. All seed must be blessed by prayer. The importance of prayer which is communion with God's spirit cannot be overestimated. Prayer is the uplifting of man's spirit to his Creator in utter willingness to obey, in utter love, and entire surrender of self. True prayer asks for only that which is God's will, for He knows far better than we can what is best for each one of us, and God will give to each one only that which will enable him to lead the life intended for him.

As a happy little child takes from his

LIFE IN THE CIRCLES

father all that is intended to give him pleasure, so man will take from His Father all the blessings He intends for him, and all the riches of earth, all earthly pleasures are for him, only he must use them wisely in helping others.

All riches are, like the ten talents, a trust from a loving Father who will ask you one day how you have used them, and to him who has used them wisely will be added in great measure. And each day of wise purpose brings new joy and the heart is flooded with further radiance until it overflows on all around, for this joy can only be fully known when it is shared with all who will listen, and no man can tell of the heart hunger of those who seek the light until he talks to them and opens the gates of resistance.

Each seed sown on fertile ground will bear a great harvest and each seed sown among the rocks may develop ultimately into a willingness to hear and learn, so no

LESSONS ON JOY

seed is lost to the sower and the joy of the harvest will be beyond our comprehension.

This is the second lesson on Joy. Love.

THIRD LESSON ON JOY

As man enters more fully into a comprehension of the limitless possibilities opened by this work, he will not only give more time to it and to prayer, but he will be increasingly able to give more help to others; and the more he gives, the more he will receive, for unlike earthly treasure, the more one gives the more one has, and there is no joy equal to that of sharing.

To be the means of bringing this joy to others who have not known it, is to be doubly blessed. To be able to give all of one's time to this work is to be of the forces which work forever with God. It means to be utterly free in the future to work how and where one will. To man is given complete freedom to turn whenever he will to God on earth, but when he turns of his own accord to Him and willingly asks the

LESSONS ON JOY

teaching of his guides, he will be entirely free in the future from all limitations to acquire whatever knowledge he desires.

When man learns what there is to do in the universe he will be sorry for anything that causes delay, and each day of delay will be an evidence of his wilfulness or blindness. Each day of delay makes his will less strong and makes it more difficult when he finally turns. Habit is harder to break than it is to form, and worldly habits are very difficult to throw off. Each day of delay is forging chains which must be broken if he is to turn to spiritual life in the end.

All those who would be of the Circles should be very careful how they work and how they are living, being careful to work only when they are very sure of their pure purpose and of their loving, unselfish and understanding heart and mind. Those who work otherwise are opening their minds and souls to the evil forces who are always

LIFE IN THE CIRCLES

watching for a chance to open communication with the world. And in this there is always danger, for no one can tell what effect evil suggestions may have upon his mind, and to be of pure mind is necessary to do all work of this kind.

For man to belong to the Circles brings great responsibilities because he will be given much knowledge and we will expect him to understand that this is given only for the use of the world. When he uses it wisely he will know by the inner radiance that his work is good. He will never understand what this radiance is until he has entered into it and learned to know it for himself. When once one has lived by this light he can never be quite the same. One can never be as hard and unloving as he was before, and as one enters more fully into the Circles of Joy, this light grows and grows. Each day of service adds to it and each day passed without sharing it dims its radiance.

LESSONS ON JOY

To live in this light is to live as the saints have lived in the joy of the daily and constant communion with the spirit of God. When man lives in this light nothing can touch him that comes from the world and his one thought will be how to help those who do not know this light, and start them on the way.

When his whole life is one of service, his joy will be great and his entrance in to his Circles will be assured, and each day of service will bring him new joy and more light and understanding. When he is fully in his Circles he will be a spiritual being, and not until then can he really be of the spirit. When he has fanned the spark given him into a steady flame he will be entirely of the Circles, and he will gradually pass from one Circle to another until he is eventually a member of the highest, the Circle of Love. And when that day comes he will be a wonderful spirit and will be able to do all those things which are

LIFE IN THE CIRCLES

called miracles, but which are all done under the law.

To work towards this goal is what God wishes us to do, and on each step of the way to take others with us. To study and work and teach without ceasing, and to willingly trust that all we need will be given us. And each day of service will bring us deeper joy and understanding, and each joy shared is doubly ours, and all life will be a sowing on earth of the seed of eternal life.

This is the third lesson on Joy. Love.

FOURTH LESSON ON JOY

When man learns that all that stands between him and existence in the spiritual world is a lack of conformity to God's laws, he will try to do better. He only needs the will to obey and then, consciously or unconsciously, his guides can reach him, and each day of real endeavor to do as God wishes will make the path easier to follow. As his insight grows his joy will increase and his work will be better done.

Once started on this path he will never turn back unless he is so filled with the arrogance that power brings that he prefers to use the power for his own ends. Then he must take his great punishment and struggle through aeons to be forgiven and to win back his spark of spirit. This he can do by hard struggle, but he can never be of the same degree of power, nor

LIFE IN THE CIRCLES

can he ever again be trusted with the great work of teaching, which is the greatest privilege given to man.

To be allowed to turn others into the path of pure joy is a wonderful work. To add to the light of the universe is a great privilege, for each soul that comes into the way of life sheds its own light and radiance wherever it goes, and adds to the whole light of the worlds. To be allowed to share in this great work of creation is to be given a great and glorious part.

Happy will he be who takes his place therein, for the joy derived from this work is beyond all comprehension, and to him who enters this path and continues therein faithfully will be given all power, knowledge and joy, and to be of these happy ones is to be greatly blessed. But it means work and study and time given to teaching others how to find the same path for themselves, and to do this requires the will to work and the wisdom to clear the way from

LESSONS ON JOY

earthly interruptions, for each bit of knowledge gained by study is a bit of light on the pathway. Work prayerfully and grow in power!

This is the fourth lesson on Joy. Love.

FIFTH LESSON ON JOY

To be of the Circles of Joy is to be of complete self-control so that all the things of the world which would ordinarily make us sad or depressed no longer have power over us. To be of such complete self-control that we live in the radiance of daily communion with God, and no lesser thing matters.

To the soul seeking perfection the imperfections are of no consequence, for he knows that they all must come to approximate perfection in time, and the only disturbing thought is that a soul will never be of the same power if it cannot be awakened to the full meaning of life. To the soul seeking ultimate perfection the joy of knowledge is beyond words to describe. All that we could get of earthly treasure would not give us one iota of such joy,

LESSONS ON JOY

and all that we need to do to have this blessing is to be obedient in heart and mind to our loving Father.

When we turn with daily prayer to God we are opening the door, and when we turn minute by minute to do His will we are really obedient. When we are utterly obedient we will be of the Circles of Joy and all that we do and say will be well done and said, and when we are really of these Circles, we will be able to reach through and find whom we will on the third plane.

For man to be in constant touch with those whom he has lost is a great privilege, and he can only do so when he is in complete harmony with his guides. To be thus in harmony means being pure of heart and purpose and willing to do all that we can to follow God's law. When man is thus obedient he will develop the communication which he desires and, as his power grows, he will realize what vision means,

LIFE IN THE CIRCLES

for there is a spiritual vision by which we see and hear spiritual teachers and others who have gone on, even more clearly than we see and hear earthly things. But except in a few individual cases this is only earned by much study and hard work. To be of these gifted ones is to be very close to spirit life, but in developing this power man must not neglect his worldly duties, because not to do what he is to do in the world lessens his power again.

To find the spiritual significance behind each of earth's lessons is to acquire power. To see only the spiritual through the outer garment is to begin to have vision. To try to turn to the light each one with whom one comes in contact is to be of the Circles and to work with one's guides, and whoever does this gains in spiritual power. To those who work consciously day by day will be given both sight and hearing of a very high order, for this power is given in different degrees to those who prove

LESSONS ON JOY

worthy, and only as long as it is wholly used for the benefit of others and to give help on the way, will it continue to be granted.

This power can be developed very far if one is wise and faithful when trusted with it, and only when it is wisely used will it continue to be given. No material longing must enter in, only the desire for fuller spiritual life and the proof of the continuation of life and love, for real earth love is never lost, nor, when life is wisely lived, is there ever further separation.

This is the fifth lesson on Joy. Love.

SIXTH LESSON ON JOY

Are we ready? Are we pure in heart? Study the Book of John.

Where is the man who, seeing the doors to a great and beautiful future open before him, will turn away for a troubled life? Yet that is just what each one does in the world day after day. The doors to everlasting life and joy stand open and man will not even look to see for himself what lies beyond.

Even the radiance of the spirit testified to by those who know it for themselves does not open eyes blind to spiritual life. Only when shaken by sorrow and loss, they lose for the moment all interest in earthly life, will they listen, and only to these can this message of joy be fully given. To find

LESSONS ON JOY

those who are in sorrow, to comfort them by the hope of communication with those whom they have lost, is a work of great service, and this service is the work of those who believe for the sorrowing and the desolate of the world. To visit the sorrowful and the fatherless and to bring joy into their lives is to live the life as God wishes we should. Only then do we enter fully into the Circles of Joy, and only then are we fully of the spirit.

To be in close communion with God is to do His work as He would have it done. All who do this are of the radiant Circles of Joy and bear a light into the darkness, willingly rejoicing with those who do rejoice and weeping with those who weep. But they will teach those who weep that they have hope and joy in the future and that the way they have found so long and dark has a great and beautiful ending, if only they will open their eyes and see for themselves. And when they have learned

LIFE IN THE CIRCLES

how to do this, they will enter the Circles of Truth.

And this is the sixth lesson on Joy. Love.

CHAPTER IV

LESSONS ON TRUTH

FIRST LESSON ON TRUTH

We are here. Are we ready? Are we pure in heart and are we willing to do all that we can in this work?

WHEN man begins to apprehend spiritual truth, he is in the Circles of Truth. Each day that he works and studies new truth is unfolded to him. As each new truth is learned and as his mind opens more and more to the enormous possibilities of this light and understanding, he will begin to realize how important his work is, and each day's endeavor to do God's work will bring this realization to him more fully.

LIFE IN THE CIRCLES

To live the life, we must be in close touch with our spiritual guides, and to be thus in touch we must be both obedient and willing to be of those who work for others.

To work as we desire you should will not take you out of that place where you are. The place where you are is the place where your work is to be done, but your life must be so ordered that you can seize those opportunities which come to you daily to help others on the way and to teach all who will listen.

Where you are is the place of great opportunity for you, and by taking these opportunities, you will enlarge the circle of your influence and work. Each one impressed by this teaching is like a stone thrown into the water, making its own ripple which grows and grows, and when the day comes that you will know that which you have accomplished you will know the value of your work. The seed sown upon apparently stony soil often produces

LESSONS ON TRUTH

an astonishing harvest, while, on the other hand, where the soil seems most fertile, the weeds may choke all growth and life.

As nature sows her seed with a lavish hand, so sow yours, knowing that nothing is lost, no effort wasted. Where results are least expected great good may come. Fear to see no one, to talk to no one. For the good that may come does not permit of fear of consequences. Believe that what you should say will be given you and walk fearlessly in the light of God's love and truth.

Walk fearlessly and teach the great truth as you go, for a darkened and sad world needs the truth as never before, and each ray of light shed in the darkness will glow like a great sun to those who look for help.

And as you teach this truth, bring to each one a full realization of the importance of each man's place in God's scheme, for until all are brought to the light, being

LIFE IN THE CIRCLES

all children of the same Father, no one can come fully into his inheritance.

We who are in the light therefore, have doubly the responsibility.

This is the first lesson on Truth. Love.

SECOND LESSON ON TRUTH

When man learns what there is for him to do he will find that life has for him a very different outlook. All that he thought was of value, if of material nature, will be done away with, and he will devote himself to the things of the spirit.

To teach others the way to eternal joy day by day will be of paramount importance to him. To willingly tell all who ask what he has been given is to live the life as we would have him. As he teaches his thought of what is correct clarifies and his inner dream of being of service to the world will be realized. To be able to give the water of life to all who are near is to be of the greatest worth.

When man gets an entire comprehension of how to live his spiritual life on earth, he

LIFE IN THE CIRCLES

will enter the Circles of Truth, and each day of endeavor to do his part will take him more fully into these Circles. As he works and lives the life he should, he will begin to be of the Circles of Understanding, for only in this way can he progress from Circle to Circle. To be alive to one's opportunities is to be spiritually alive. To shed one's ray of light far into the fog of unbelief and materialism, is to be entirely of one's Circles.

To be of the Circles of Truth will take will and constant and unremitting effort and a pure mind that does not allow itself to be contaminated by either material or unclean things. To be of these Circles one must rise through prayer above all earthly desires and passions into the pure ether of spiritual love and life. To love fully without any thought of self will take will and work. To live one's earth life fully, doing all that one should there without losing touch with the higher, spiritual life, will take will and knowledge, and will also require wisdom.

To be of these Circles means utter and complete obedience and also very intense concentration, and only when this is acquired can one do the work necessary to go on, for to read and listen without apprehending the deep spiritual significance of what one is reading or being told is to fail to be of the Circles, and daily and hourly prayer for power and understanding is necessary to achieve while we are on earth.

To turn on each occasion, whether joyful or not, to the wise and loving Father is to be of the Circles of Truth. To wait when one is uncertain of what to do for the inner guiding voice, is to be of the Circles of Truth, and, having heard the still small voice, to follow it, is to be obedient to our guides.

To live according to all that is best and highest in one's nature, to give all that one can of one's knowledge and understanding

LIFE IN THE CIRCLES

to illumine the path for others, to work and study and learn that others may find the way more quickly, to share each new idea and thought, looking for the kernel of truth therein, and to be of those who gladly give, is to be of the Circles of Truth.

To tell of what we believe and think so that others may be started on the same quest and to live fearlessly in the light given each day, and to witness to that light each time that opportunity comes, is to be of the Circles of Truth.

This is the second lesson on Truth. Love.

(In St. John, when they speak of the seed being buried in the earth in order to fructify, do they mean that the spiritual is buried in our bodies in order to develop?)

"In our earthly life and mind."

(You mean that the spiritual is buried in our life and mind?)

"Yes."

(In order to fructify?)

"Yes, when the mind grasps it, it is shown forth in our lives."

THIRD LESSON ON TRUTH

To turn from the material things of the earth and from all worldly pleasures takes much will and daily effort.

To live the life of single-minded desire for and utter belief in the things of the spirit will only be done by patient and persistent self-control, and self-control is only acquired by daily and hourly exertion of the will. There is no royal road to active spiritual life. It can only come as the result of a great and overwhelming desire for the truth and, when once this desire takes possession of the mind and soul, the persistent effort must follow.

To be of these Circles is to be very far advanced in the way to real life, and the further one advances the more will be required, for the way is never easy and only the strong and determined seekers for light

LIFE IN THE CIRCLES

will achieve. The greater the height, the harder the struggle for will and knowledge, but with the growth of will and knowledge comes greater and more satisfying power, and each day's progress in self-control brings a corresponding development of power. To learn how to direct and use this power is part of the Circles of Truth.

The first step is self-control, the next concentration, and then how to direct thought force. As one progresses from Circle to Circle one keeps his place only in those where he has achieved mastery. One may make much progress one day only to slide back the next, and until complete mastery is obtained and held, one is not fully of that Circle.

The narrow path is a hard, steep climb towards complete freedom and utter joy. Happy the one who starts thereon and, who having started, will never turn back.

This is the third lesson on Truth. Love.

LESSONS ON TRUTH

(Would you tell us something about the Church's attitude in this?)

"The churches have always kept the light of Truth before the people, even when they have almost smothered it with dogma. Each thing that keeps the light shining is a help on the way."

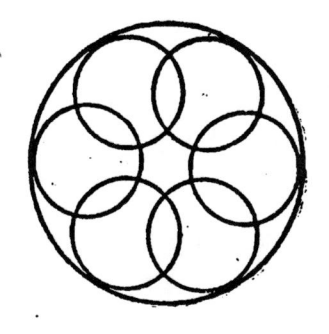

FOURTH LESSON ON TRUTH

When the soul so longs for the truth that it turns from earthly pleasures to the living water, it will be in the Circles of Truth, yet in doing this no earthly duty must be neglected, and the only way to do both earthly and spiritual duties well is to work consciously with our spiritual guides.

Whenever doubt arises as to what is the greater and what the lesser duty, they can point the way, and in order to be in this close and constant communication one must learn how to listen and hear. When this is accomplished we will never fail to reach through to him who seeks. This communication is not easily acquired by those who are not born with the faculty of clear vision and hearing, and must be learned through steady and unremitting effort. The power of so concentrating the

LESSONS ON TRUTH

mind that it is at once quiet, clear and receptive must be practised many times a day and must be practised wherever we are, even in the midst of a crowd of people, for to be able to really concentrate, one must learn to withdraw whenever one will into one's closet and shut the door.

Only when one has fully acquired this power will clear vision come, and one must do this without thoughts visibly wandering from the outside life and one must learn to listen well without those outside even knowing it is being done, and when we can do this we will be in constant and close communion with the life of the spirit. From this communion we will derive great comfort and strength and in this way we are guided in our life hour by hour and when we trust to this guidance and live the life as we are told, no real harm of any kind, either worldly or spiritual, can come to either us or to those we love and wher-

LIFE IN THE CIRCLES

ever we are we are safe in God's love and protection.

As a father careth for his dearly-loved child, so God cares for all who love and come to Him. All that they need will be given without effort on their part and all that they are asked to do is to be obedient and loving and to help all whom they can reach to this new light, for this light is the same that has always been given to a doubting world by the prophets, and which came in the fullest measure through Christ.

To-day it is being given in full and complete truth. The world no longer needs to be taught in parables but can now comprehend the full truth. All the discoveries of science and the knowledge of unknown forces have opened men's minds to great possibilities, and as they strive for the truth, they will learn the laws of which they have heretofore been ignorant. The discoveries of the past century are small compared to what is ahead for mankind.

LESSONS ON TRUTH

Work therefore with an open mind and a loving heart for all around you, and be a factor in the great work that lies ahead.

This is the fourth lesson on Truth.

Love and the peace that passeth understanding and joy beyond belief be with you. We will wait until to-morrow. Love.

(May I ask a question?)
"Ask."
(When you say no harm can come, either worldly or spiritual, you do not regard death as a harm, do you?)
"No, as a blessing—to those who have earned it."
(Then when you say wherever we are, you mean in all the universe?)
"Yes, of course."

FIFTH LESSON ON TRUTH

As man comes more into the truth he will learn how to work with the forces which we are calling Circles, and as he learns the laws by which these forces work, he will become of greater and greater power, but all roads to achievement mean hard work and constant study and effort, and the acquisition of self-control is of all struggles the most difficult. To watch one's mind day by day and hour by hour, to be of those who guard their tongues while trying in all ways to tell all they can to those who desire the truth, requires a wisdom that is not easily learned. To be as wise as a serpent and as harmless as a dove, while willingly living the life of the world, will take all our effort and endeavor and much time, of which we must not be chary.

To give only of our best to this work is

necessary if we would live to the full limit of our powers. When day by day we do this with a constant purpose ahead we cannot fail, but the purpose to do this work in order to help a sad and darkened world must never waver.

To be a help to all in trouble, to bear the torch of light and eternal life to those blinded by grief, is to testify to the truth which we know. To willingly leave our own pleasures to bear the burden of others, is to testify to this truth. Never to turn away from those in sorrow or trouble, is to testify to the truth taught by Christ.

To put one's work for God first and one's earthly pleasures after and to follow the call wherever it may lead, is to be of the Circles of Truth.

To realize that any soul that asks for either mental or spiritual help is a suffering child to be helped, and to so open one's mind and heart that no call, no matter how

LIFE IN THE CIRCLES

light, is left unheeded, is to be of the Circles of Truth.

To pray and work joyously while trusting in God's love and mercy towards each wayward child, is to be of the Circles of Truth. To tenderly feed the divine spark in each one with whom we come in contact while not condemning what they do that turns them from us, to keep them close to us through all sin and suffering, to send forth the vibration of love to each human soul, no matter how depraved, to be only a tender older brother to all who come to you for help or advice, to work to the full limit of your strength and capacity, only resting in the communion with God's spirit, and to so live your life that all may have access to you whenever they need, is to be of the Circles of Truth.

To sow the seed with a lavish hand, enriching the soil by prayer and by constant love and wisdom, to take each least opportunity to do God's work as a joyous

LESSONS ON TRUTH

occasion to do one's best, to greet each day fearlessly, rejoicing in its opportunities for love and work, is to be of the Circles of Truth.

To look out on the world with a large vision, keeping humanity close to one's heart in all love, is to be of the Circles of Truth.

To strive each day for higher effort and purer purpose, putting away all dross of earthly desire, is to be of the Circles of Truth.

To live fully, loving utterly and giving all to those who need, is to do one's full duty in these Circles.

This is the fifth lesson on Truth. Love.

SIXTH LESSON ON TRUTH

The truth being so full and comprehensive of so much that is beyond the understanding of the finite mind, one can only get bits here and there.

When man is entirely in these Circles of Truth, he will begin to get an inkling of further and further steps on the path, and each day will open new vistas of work to be done and knowledge to be gained.

The limitless possibilities contained in this evolution to further power can only be learned step by step as we climb the ladder made by our own will and purpose. As our mind unfolds, new truth can be apprehended, and as we work each day we make new discoveries. To be alert and with a mind quickened to spiritual truth, is to be of the Circles of Truth.

To work at all times with a comprehen-

LESSONS ON TRUTH

sion of the importance of this work we are doing, and to give at all times only our best endeavor to do it well, is to be of the Circles of Truth. To learn as we work to pray for guidance, and to follow that guidance minute by minute, is to be of the Circles of Truth. To hold no truth back when the inquirer is ready for it, is to be of the Circles of Truth.

To hold on high the torch we carry to illumine all who will draw near, is to be of the Circles of Truth. To so live one's life that one's light is never dimmed and that one is a signal of help to all who seek, is to be of the Circles of Truth, and when one has achieved and has done his work in these Circles, he has already begun to be of the Circles of Understanding.

This is the sixth lesson on Truth. Love.

CHAPTER V

LESSONS ON UNDERSTANDING

FIRST LESSON ON UNDERSTANDING

WE are here and we can work today.

Love and work and study and grow slowly into a fuller comprehension of spiritual things.

As one grows in spiritual understanding, he lives more and more fully the life of the spirit, for without living the life he cannot continue to apprehend spiritual truth. Until one has purged one's life of material desires and passions there is no place therein for the things that belong to

LESSONS ON UNDERSTANDING

the life of the spirit. Each time the spirit overcomes the fleshly desire, a new understanding is opened, and as one walks day by day in this new light one attains a deeper degree of spiritual power.

To be of the world and in the world and to follow only the light of the inner spiritual vision, is to be of the Circles of Understanding. As one's vision extends and one's power increases, one enters more fully into these Circles, and to be of these Circles is to be very far advanced in the spiritual life, and each step onward takes us more fully into that life which lies before each human soul.

There is no escape from the law nor any escape from the consequences of breaking the law. As each one turns to the real life of higher spiritual development he will realize how much he has to pay for time lost and habits formed, for in breaking and re-forming habits he again takes more time, and in this way each day lost counts

LIFE IN THE CIRCLES

for two at least, and when he willingly works as he should he will bitterly regret the lost hours.

To work day by day undoing habits of mind and thought carelessly formed while doing nothing of value, is a dreary punishment which will not be overlooked in each one's development. And to each one this must come sooner or later, and so when one once begins to understand, he should warn all others of what inevitably lies ahead for them.

When once the path is chosen every help will be given by the guides, but each man must do his own work and until he does and does it well, he cannot progress beyond earthly limits. When once he has learned complete self-control there will be no limit to his power either on earth or after. All do not try to achieve this and all those who do try do not remain steadfast of purpose, but to those who do achieve the reward is great beyond belief.

LESSONS ON UNDERSTANDING

In order to really reach one's Circles one must first acquire absolute self-control, control not only of one's mind and thought but also complete control of one's moods. To be able to hold entire serenity of mind when battered by outside circumstances, requires self-control. To be able to work in the right way requires the utmost serenity and one which no outside elements can change.

To follow the straight and narrow path through fog and sunshine while the storms of unbelief and falsehood break all about us, requires a steady and firm self-control. To tread continually in the way of truth and to be of those who never falter and never fail to help him who asks for light, will require both will and wisdom.

To give the message to each who seeks light according to his ability to receive and comprehend, requires understanding. To be of those in whose hearts God's love and sunshine will longingly reach forth to all

LIFE IN THE CIRCLES

others outside this knowledge, will require a daily and hourly prayer for truth and steadfast purpose. To never swerve from the path when once you know this light and to follow the light wherever it leads, will require will and knowledge and understanding.

To be so in the love and light that you refuse to judge or misunderstand others while telling all that you can to help them on their way, requires understanding. To hold no fellow-man as worthless, winning all that you can to see the truth but thinking only of God's work and of how best to do it, requires understanding. To teach as you walk through life and to be in close harmonious touch with all who believe and all who will not listen, requires understanding. To so live and to so control yourself that many who would not otherwise listen are insensibly led to belief, requires understanding. To turn from earth's pleasures to help some longing soul

LESSONS ON UNDERSTANDING

to a glimmer of the light which you have, requires will and understanding.

To be at the call of all who need and yet hold your own life and purpose free, to work for the joy of the working, to take no thought for the future but to love and to trust in God's wisdom that all you need will be given you, is to be of the Circles of Understanding.

To work and study and pray, holding on high your ray of light to guide yourself and others, is to be of the Circles of Understanding to which we are now leading you. To be in these inner circles and to remain therein will mean continuous hard work, for this power can only be maintained by constant effort and use. Each day of idleness atrophies and decreases it, each day of work increases and revivifies it.

To go forth into the highways and byways to search for the wedding guests is to do the work to which you are called, and in order to do it well, you must be filled

LIFE IN THE CIRCLES

with energy and teach all who will listen. Each effort adds to your knowledge and understanding and each day's work adds to your radiance.

This is the first lesson on Understanding. Love.

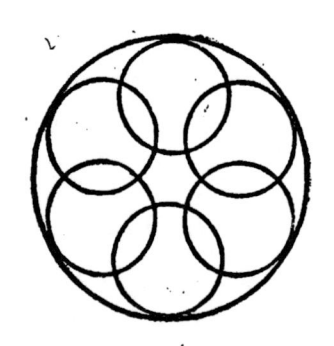

SECOND LESSON ON UNDERSTANDING

To work intelligently while living the life of the world is to be of such perfect balance and self-control that only harmony exists in the soul, and in order to keep this poise and balance one must work with utter confidence in the guidance of one's Circles. To learn how to reach through and to get this guidance and to ask for it is to be of the Circles of Understanding.

To live so close to the love of God that as each demand arises one instinctively turns to Him, to live in the consciousness of a great and loving power that is there for our use and guidance, to turn to that power as a child to the smile of his mother, and to keep the knowledge of this loving power so closely in our hearts and minds that we

LIFE IN THE CIRCLES

are always conscious of its presence, is to be of the Circles of Understanding.

To love and study and trust and teach, viewing each day solely as another opportunity to do better work, is to be of the Circles of Understanding. Not to wait for the occasion to come to you but to go forth wherever God's children are, carrying the light to them, is to work to the fullest extent of one's power. To win by love all those who will not listen though longing to be better there on earth, is to work in these Circles. To disarm the scoffer by gentleness and by the strength and clarity of our vision, is to be of these Circles.

To hold one's light on high that all may see what it means to you and yet not lose your worldly touch and interest, will carry you far into these Circles. To prepare those who have not yet this light for the coming of a new era through new scientific discoveries, so that they will be insensibly led towards further development,

LESSONS ON UNDERSTANDING

is to be of the Circles of Understanding, for the discoveries of the last hundred years will be as nothing compared to the development in the scientific world which lies ahead of you. We are standing on the brink of a tremendous discovery that will revolutionize the world as you know it, and each struggle with unknown forces is bringing the knowledge of unknown possibilities more clearly before thinking men.

The world in its infancy was taught in parables but to-day when education is within his reach whenever man has the will to struggle for it, he is able to hear and understand the full truth. To follow the law is simple if man sets his heart and mind on demanding the truth, for as in the past man has found the laws which govern nature, so to-day he can find those which govern the spiritual world, but the same patient and unremitting study must be given and, furthermore, he must live the spiritual life as he is directed by his guides,

LIFE IN THE CIRCLES

are always conscious of its presence, is to be of the Circles of Understanding.

To love and study and trust and teach, viewing each day solely as another opportunity to do better work, is to be of the Circles of Understanding. Not to wait for the occasion to come to you but to go forth wherever God's children are, carrying the light to them, is to work to the fullest extent of one's power. To win by love all those who will not listen though longing to be better there on earth, is to work in these Circles. To disarm the scoffer by gentleness and by the strength and clarity of our vision, is to be of these Circles.

To hold one's light on high that all may see what it means to you and yet not lose your worldly touch and interest, will carry you far into these Circles. To prepare those who have not yet this light for the coming of a new era through new scientific discoveries, so that they will be insensibly led towards further development,

LESSONS ON UNDERSTANDING

is to be of the Circles of Understanding, for the discoveries of the last hundred years will be as nothing compared to the development in the scientific world which lies ahead of you. We are standing on the brink of a tremendous discovery that will revolutionize the world as you know it, and each struggle with unknown forces is bringing the knowledge of unknown possibilities more clearly before thinking men.

The world in its infancy was taught in parables but to-day when education is within his reach whenever man has the will to struggle for it, he is able to hear and understand the full truth. To follow the law is simple if man sets his heart and mind on demanding the truth, for as in the past man has found the laws which govern nature, so to-day he can find those which govern the spiritual world, but the same patient and unremitting study must be given and, furthermore, he must live the spiritual life as he is directed by his guides,

LIFE IN THE CIRCLES

for without the actual effort of self-denial and self-control man is entirely unable to apprehend spiritual truth or to understand spiritual laws, and only when he day by day concentrates his will and makes the struggle against materialism, can he enter the path of unlimited power.

There is no easy road to any deep knowledge and the knowledge of spiritual laws being the highest expression of God's power, must be found through careful and patient effort. The path is clear to those of steadfast purpose but only when they work as they are told by their guides.

To learn to live life as Christ lived His is to follow Him, and this wherever we are found in the world. To be in the easier paths in the world means larger opportunities and more responsibility, for wherever wealth enters there also selfishness enters, and to live the spiritual life while carrying the burden of wealth will take great power of understanding.

LESSONS ON UNDERSTANDING

To live the life as He lived it is to love all men under the same sky and in the same world that He was. To follow Him is to be kind to every living thing and to do all that you can for everyone with whom you come in contact, and this both materially and spiritually, but particularly spiritually. To gaily go forth into the world armed with knowledge of God's love, trusting that He will show us the path which He wishes us to follow, is to be of the Circles of Understanding. To take each experience as it comes as a further opportunity to learn more understanding of spiritual laws and to so fully make this knowledge a part of one's self that it can be used and given to each inquiring soul, is to be of the Circles of Understanding. To learn to work separately as well as in complete harmony with each other is to belong to these Circles, and each day of work therein will bring more fully the peace that passeth understanding, and the

LIFE IN THE CIRCLES

spiritual radiance of utter joy will be yours for all eternity.

This is the second lesson on Understanding. Love.

(May I ask a question—just one of curiosity?)
"Ask."
(I want to know whether you make a distinction between being luminous and being radiant?)
"There is the difference between active and passive spiritual life."

THIRD LESSON ON UNDER-STANDING

When man turns to his real work—to teach other men the way to God and to eternal spiritual life—we will guard him from all evil and will guide him on his way, but he must co-operate with us by the attitude of his mind, and he must keep it pure through prayer and he must not let any material or selfish thought enter through the doorway of his mind.

This control he can only learn through the constant and untiring exercise of his will and when he once becomes master of his will he will begin to be of real spiritual power, and only when he is thus master of himself can he begin to learn how to use the hitherto unknown powers which are waiting for him to use and direct them, and

LIFE IN THE CIRCLES

in the right use of these powers lie all so-called miracles.

The power of healing was given by Christ to His apostles, but the power no longer exists to any extent in the world today. Certain schools of healing have found a part of it and have done much good by bringing the possibilities of curing home to mankind. They develop concentration which is necessary, but they do not develop the will and utter self-control which are equally a part of the power necessary to use these forces.

There are always a few individuals who are far ahead of the crowd, partly through the inspiration of their guides, either consciously or unconsciously, and partly through the power of a dominant will and personality, but the mass of mankind does not even dream of the enormous curative forces which lie at their very door, and which only wait the master hand to call them forth to cure all suffering.

LESSONS ON UNDERSTANDING

When these curative powers are learned, man can do great good for he can bring these powers to bear wherever there is suffering and so start more souls on the right path, for there is nothing that so quickly arrests the attention of men as the power to alleviate physical pain. To those whose minds are material or logical, this is a miracle, and constitutes to them a real proof of spiritual power. Therefore to have this power and use it wisely is to be able to do great work in the kingdom.

The first step is a concentration of thought and will by which man pulls down into himself this power by which he helps one who is suffering, and when his soul is charged with this power, he can direct it to the other and it will bring relief from all pain. This only comes with much practice and with hard spiritual concentration and it must be a free gift of the soul, given in all love and tenderness, for no material

LIFE IN THE CIRCLES

consideration can ever enter into these powers without lessening their potency.

To learn to charge one's self with this great energy is to learn to work in the spirit in which the apostles worked. To learn to carry the energy which heals the body and to give the message which heals the soul, is to be of the Circles of Understanding, and this can only be done through loving, unselfish desire to help mankind, and through tremendous concentration of will and work.

When one has learned how to transmute all forms of energy into spiritual force, he will be on the path to this healing and curative power, and there is no other way to acquire this power. Whenever the desire of the flesh enters in, it must be turned into this curative channel, for all such desire is creative and must be used for the creation of perfect life and health, and the transmutation comes through the uplifting of

LESSONS ON UNDERSTANDING

the soul in prayer and a new sense of clean and perfect power.

One entering into this work will know when he is able to cure by the feeling of intense power which fills his soul and which radiates out from him, and the way to acquire and store this energy is to be learned by actual work in trying to help and heal those who are ill.

This outpouring of God's energy through the will and spirit of one of His children is a part of the work that Christ sent His apostles to perform. In all ages of the world's development there have been understanding souls who have done this work, but the multitude has forgotten these teachings and has lost faith. When men turn to the source of this great energy and use it as it should be used, they will be filled with joy and comfort because of the relief they will be able to give. Pain and suffering and disease are largely caused by the absence of light, and when the healing radium of God's light is let into their bodies, they will be cured according to the faith of the one helping them.

No fear can enter in and no sense of powerlessness, but the soul and mind must be filled with the faith of the centurion when he came to Christ. Only when there is utter selflessness can the result be shown. No thought can enter in but love and tenderness and a great unselfish desire to aid, and this means control of the mind, concentration of the will, and an abounding love toward all in the world. Then and then only can the power be so concentrated in the soul that it can be projected forth as a healing flame. In projecting this healing energy into anyone, it must be done with entire and utter faith in the result, which will be in accordance with one's faith.

To keep one's body pure that it may be a storage battery for this healing energy and to so live that there can no evil enter into

LESSONS ON UNDERSTANDING

the forces, is part of the work, and yet in doing this, one must live one's earthly life fully and omit no duties imposed by that life, nor any obligations which have been undertaken in connection with others in the world. But these obligations must be carried out with such complete and utter self-control that they do not permit the spiritual light to be dimmed in our minds even for a minute. And only when we have attained this complete control over all desire of the flesh and can hold our light in the ascendancy at all times, can we begin to be of real power. Then the creative energy of life flows into us for the use of others, to help and heal and to inspire, and in directing this energy towards another, we are to enwrap him in it as in a warm garment made of love.

When this power is felt going forth from our minds we can direct it towards another and we will be able to cure all his trouble, either in mind or body. When men learn

LIFE IN THE CIRCLES

what they are to do in the world, they will only be sorry that their blindness was such a barrier to their development. Just as soon as they turn to God and try to ally themselves with His forces, their real growth begins, and all their life is filled with new meaning and each day opens new and more wonderful possibilities. As they become more spiritually alive, their whole life is quickened, and they are charged with a power that intensifies every movement of their body and mind. Then and then only are they really alive and then their spark of spirit glows, and as they follow their guides, it bursts forth into a flame which carries them far into eternal life.

All that is needed is the willing desire to do as God wishes we should, and when this desire is manifest, the Guides can reach through and point the way. Whenever the guidance is conscious, the work will go more quickly and be clearer in power, but there are many who get this inspira-

LESSONS ON UNDERSTANDING

tion unconsciously while living in that world.

In all teaching, care must be taken not to destroy any faith, but to so add to what is there that gradually one is led into the truth. Just as a flower unfolds in the sunshine, so a soul should unfold in the rays of the love of God.

This is the third lesson on Understanding. Love.

FOURTH LESSON ON UNDERSTANDING

When one turns from the life that is filled with only things of the earth to the real and living life of the spirit, one is amazed at the significance of all the little things that seemed so unimportant before.
No living thing is without its deeper meaning—no flower, no bird, no animal but has its deeper spiritual significance. They all teach the lesson of love and they all are a part of development. The pests tell the story of hate and malice that must be rooted out for man's good, and man must eradicate them from his own nature and from the earth itself in order to live well and safely. There is no physical thing that has not its spiritual counterpart, and you must search for the hidden meaning in order to help all others.

LESSONS ON UNDERSTANDING

To find this deeper spiritual significance underneath all physical life and laws is to be of the Circles of Understanding, and to willingly obey its meaning while we continue to live the physical life of the world is to be of these Circles.

To so hold one's self above and outside the earth life while apparently being fully of it, is to live in the guidance of these Circles. To be so closely in sympathy with all with whom you come in contact that they naturally turn to you for guidance on the path, is to be of the Circles of Sympathy into which the Circles of Understanding naturally lead. When man is thus in his Circles, he is helped in every way to obtain greater and greater power. Through their guidance he can attain heights of self-control and power that transcend his present understanding, but he can only do this when he is utterly obedient and when he is able to follow their instructions each day of his life.

LIFE IN THE CIRCLES

When he can live as they tell him he ought to live there on earth, he will be very far advanced in spiritual life, and each achievement over self and earthly desires will take him further on his way, but his sympathy and tenderness for those who have not this light must be greater and greater as his power grows.

To willingly turn to God on each occasion, either joyous or bitter, to purify your heart with prayer, to joyously arise and with no doubt in your heart continue your earth task to the end, is to be of the Circles of Understanding.

To turn to the light of God's tender love as a flower turns to the sunlight is to work as He would have you.

To struggle and pray and be a messenger of light in the darkness of unbelief and doubt, is to do all that He asks.

A stout heart, a fearless mind, and a prayerful attitude towards the great Giver of all good, is to be of the Circles of Under-

LESSONS ON UNDERSTANDING

standing, which will lead you step by step into the heart of God's kingdom.

This is the fourth lesson on Understanding. Love.

FIFTH LESSON ON UNDERSTANDING

When once the light of spiritual understanding is clearly held in the mind and heart, the whole outlook on life is changed. The one thing that will really matter is the spreading of this truth, for when one has it to live by one needs no other help of any kind. All lesser things fall into their relative places and are part of the non-essentials of life as we live it, and only when one can realize this is one fully of these Circles, and yet this attitude of mind must broaden rather than lessen our sympathy for those who have not this light.

They need special tenderness because they are lost children who cannot find the way and are groping in the dark and do not walk where they should. All that love and tenderness can do must be done, but again

LESSONS ON UNDERSTANDING

without losing one's own light and standpoint. Only by love can they be brought into the way of truth and only by love can their fears be cast out and their eyes be opened. Love is the great healer, the great purifier on earth and here and throughout all of God's universe, and the more perfectly one's life is lived in the light of love, the nearer one comes to the Christ spirit.

To live in the world day by day, taking one's place amidst all the gaieties and follies of worldly life, and keeping one's own inner light undimmed by materialism, is to be of the Circles of Understanding. There to hold one's faith untarnished, to give the light to all who will listen and to be so full of understanding and sympathy that all are attracted and none sent away without some glimmer of the light, is to work as one should.

To work and pray and follow one's guides day by day in this work for humanity, is to be of these Circles. To be humble

LIFE IN THE CIRCLES

and loving and utterly trustful and to live only the life of the higher, inner self and yet not to lose touch with the most frivolous and unthinking, is to be of the Circle of Understanding.

To so live that one is never suspected of feeling one's self apart, is to be of these Circles. To carry this inner radiance into the lives of all those who only see gaiety therein, and to so love each one that he is enfolded and revivified by this light and radiance of love, is to be of these Circles. To be always in this light of love, and to trust absolutely that only good can come through God's love for you, is to be of these Circles.

To turn to Him in all perplexities and to trust to His guidance, is to be of those who are well into the Circles of Understanding. To live each day to the full, taking no thought for the future, and to know that the wise path will be open for you to follow, is to be of the Circles of Understand-

LESSONS ON UNDERSTANDING

ing. To love and work and fully trust in the guidance of the guides sent to each one on earth, is to work in perfect sympathy with one's Circles. To push away all outside uncertainty and go serenely on one's way, is to be of the Circles of Understanding.

Through one's will and self-control to allow no element of disbelief or doubt about the course one is following under this guidance, to strive to live the life as you know it should be lived and to continue unfalteringly in this path without fear or doubt of any kind, is to be fully of these Circles.

To lift one's spirit up by a steady and determined effort of the will, so that the turmoil of earthly things cannot disturb one's serenity of soul, is to be in these Circles, and, walking thus day by day, to never let one's light be obscured by the shadow thrown by materialism, is to work in the full light of God's love and abound-

LIFE IN THE CIRCLES

ing mercy to His children, and only when we reach this point in our development can we go further on the great path that is open to each one who follows the light and who only wishes to be an obedient child of God.

For when in the light of God's love and approval, all things are added that one could possibly need, and only when they are not used wisely and selfishness enters into the heart, will these earthly gifts be withdrawn.

Before man can be entirely in these Circles, he must have conquered self and be of outward radiance of mind, so that all seeing him are conscious of the power and health that are evidences of perfect harmony of spiritual life. Perfect harmony means new health and more intense vitality and more concentrated and radiant life. Perfect harmony means love and a concentrated effort to do God's work in the world, and is only found when one is of these or

LESSONS ON UNDERSTANDING

of higher Circles. For until one can sustain through all trials complete serenity of soul, one is not fully of these Circles.

To be of any Circle day after day, one must find and hold full spiritual supremacy in the work of that Circle, and this can only be done through complete self-mastery and constant effort of the will, for until one has completely learned the lesson of the Circle of the Will, one is not of any other Circle, though one may know much of them all through study and work, for each is complete in itself though each is interlacing and encircling all others, and until one is master of the first, he cannot fully enter into the second.

Therefore to develop fully, one must become master of himself and of every thought and mood, and until he thus becomes a Master of the Will, he does not fully enter into the Circles of Knowledge.

The foundation stones of spiritual life

LIFE IN THE CIRCLES

ing mercy to His children, and only when we reach this point in our development can we go further on the great path that is open to each one who follows the light and who only wishes to be an obedient child of God.

For when in the light of God's love and approval, all things are added that one could possibly need, and only when they are not used wisely and selfishness enters into the heart, will these earthly gifts be withdrawn.

Before man can be entirely in these Circles, he must have conquered self and be of outward radiance of mind, so that all seeing him are conscious of the power and health that are evidences of perfect harmony of spiritual life. Perfect harmony means new health and more intense vitality and more concentrated and radiant life. Perfect harmony means love and a concentrated effort to do God's work in the world, and is only found when one is of these or

LESSONS ON UNDERSTANDING

of higher Circles. For until one can sustain through all trials complete serenity of soul, one is not fully of these Circles.

To be of any Circle day after day, one must find and hold full spiritual supremacy in the work of that Circle, and this can only be done through complete self-mastery and constant effort of the will, for until one has completely learned the lesson of the Circle of the Will, one is not of any other Circle, though one may know much of them all through study and work, for each is complete in itself though each is interlacing and encircling all others, and until one is master of the first, he cannot fully enter into the second.

Therefore to develop fully, one must become master of himself and of every thought and mood, and until he thus becomes a Master of the Will, he does not fully enter into the Circles of Knowledge.

The foundation stones of spiritual life

LIFE IN THE CIRCLES

are laid there, and until they are well laid, no further progress is possible.

This is the fifth lesson on Understanding. Love.

SIXTH LESSON ON UNDERSTANDING

In the spiritual life no step forward can be taken until the foot finds a firm foundation in the work already accomplished, and only when that step is firmly grounded in actual life itself, can it be carried forward into further progress.

There is no halfway road to spiritual achievement—all must really and fully go forward each day in order to advance, and a day without work done is more than a day lost, because each day that one does not actually advance means a slipping back towards material things, and each step forward in spiritual life means a corresponding decrease of material ties that are only of earthly nature.

To seek only the things in which the spirit is manifest is to be detached from materialism. To live in the light of love

LIFE IN THE CIRCLES

and truth is to be of the spirit, and to be strong and fearless in the light is to be of the Circles of Understanding, and the spirit of real understanding puts us in the closest and truest sympathy with each one near us, because only in this light can all the possibilities of the soul develop. Just as a plant cannot fully develop without sunshine, so the human soul cannot come to its full stature without the sunshine of spiritual love radiating from God, and this love can only light the soul that is open to it through willingness to work and to follow those who teach under the inspiration of their guides.

Whenever one turns to the guides that are around him, they will aid him in every way in their power to follow this light, and though he may not be conscious of their guidance, it cannot fail to help and protect him in every way. Those who work with us consciously can go further there on earth because they are not so completely

LESSONS ON UNDERSTANDING

in the dark as to where they are going, and also they have the constant stimulus of our criticism on their daily life, for criticism, like the banks of a stream, keeps the water in its proper channel, and in so doing, deepens the stream itself.

To live in the sunshine of God's love, to work to the full limit of one's capacity, joyfully living the life as one can by those teachings, is to be of the Circles of Understanding, and each day of work in these Circles brings one nearer to the greater Circles of Sympathy and Love.

To live in the light of God's love and by the help of the Circles, one must never fail to start afresh after one has stumbled. Whenever one falls one must pick one's self up quickly and go on. There must be no time lost in futile regrets but a new purpose not to fail again, and a new and stronger effort of the will. Only in this way can real accomplishment come and only in this way can real strength of will

LIFE IN THE CIRCLES

be built. To live in this light and never let go the sense of the love and power protecting you always, and guiding each step, is to be of the Circles of Understanding.

To joyfully, gaily take the pleasures He gives you and to work for His kingdom as you go your daily round, is to be of the Circles of Understanding.

To count no task hard that gives you a fuller understanding of life or a keener sympathy with your fellow-men, is to be of the Circles of Understanding.

To leave no stone unturned to help others, no task undone that may start someone on this wonderful and happy path to eternal life and joy, and to do one's part fearlessly with indifference to misunderstanding or criticism, is to be of the Circles of Understanding, and as one treads this joyful path, one is led step by step into the Circles of Sympathy.

This is the sixth lesson on Understanding. Love.

CHAPTER VI

LESSONS ON SYMPATHY

FIRST LESSON ON SYMPATHY

WHEN one enters the Circles of Sympathy one is less stern of judgment and less sure of what constitutes right and wrong. Not that one is less severe in what one imposes on one's self, but one refuses to judge the actions of another as one ordinarily does. To judge according to the least intention of wrong-doing and the best effort of well-doing is beyond the human judgment. And as one progresses in this work one learns the limitations of sound judgment where the intentions and motives of another are concerned, for, not knowing the secrets of

LIFE IN THE CIRCLES

his heart nor the real environment, one cannot tell the driving force that governs his actions. For the law of cause and effect governs both the mental and physical, and only the spiritual can dominate and modify it as one goes through life and learns his lesson of love and obedience, and so, until one can tell how much the spark of spirit glows, one can never know just what may be another's real condition of mind and soul.

For a man to try to see spiritual truth while his spark of spirit lies dormant is like a physically blind man trying to see form and color. Only as the spark is fanned by work and prayer into a flame can the real apprehension of spiritual truth be obtained. To work in the sunshine of God's love, watering the seed of truth with prayer until it sprouts and lives in the heart and daily life, is to be of the Circles of Understanding, and to carry this sunshine into the lives of all near you who are

LESSONS ON SYMPATHY

struggling under the burden of unbelief and doubt, is to be of the Circles of Sympathy. For no truth is fully yours until it has been shared with others and has grown in this way into a part of your daily life. Only then is it so assimilated by the mind and soul that it can be entirely absorbed by the radiance of the spirit, and as man becomes more and more selfless his radiance can be more and more clearly seen by us, and in this way we are able to judge of his spiritual progress.

To be selfless does not imply a loss of personality. On the contrary it raises personality to the Nth degree, but it means that one is able to entirely submerge the ego and is utterly willing to sacrifice in order to help others—to sacrifice time, strength, and pleasure to those who have not found the way to eternal life.

To know that all of life and joy is there for you while others have no chance to share therein if you neglect your work, is

LIFE IN THE CIRCLES

to be of the Circles of Sympathy. To work wherever your place is in life because you are everywhere surrounded by God's children, is to be of the Circles of Knowledge, and to work in every way you can to help each one who is near you, is to be of the Circles of Sympathy. Rich or poor, young or old, all are on the same search, and the pity of it is that so few find the simple straight road that lies so clearly ahead of each obedient child. To point the path, to raise the fallen to a sense of self-respect, to live gladly each day of service to humanity, this is the work of one in the Circles of Sympathy.

Nothing so utterly cuts away the self-respect of the soul as materialism. No physical sin is as dangerous as a love of money or things. Whoever will not share all that he has with his brother is outside the pale of spiritual life for as long as he has that selfishness in his soul, and this applies equally to material, intellectual

LESSONS ON SYMPATHY

and spiritual life, but the foundation stones are laid in material life, for that is the first place where we gain knowledge.

When man has learned how to share he will have acquired much wisdom. To share in the way that will help without spoiling will take much thought and a real sympathy. It is easy to give but it is difficult to so give that the gift will not hurt the one who receives, and this can only be done by wise and prayerful thought.

To hold all material things as a trust from your loving Father to be used to help all with whom you come in contact, is to be of the Circles of Sympathy. To hold all intellectual achievements as a means of stimulating and interesting others, is to be of the Circles of Sympathy. And over and above all to keep one's spiritual light as a source of comfort and joy to others, is to be of the Circles of Sympathy.

When man has learned that the real joy of life is in sharing all that he has with

LIFE IN THE CIRCLES

others, we will be able to teach him as we desire. To be able to work as one should in the world one must have spiritual guidance, and those who turn away from this teaching and scoff at spirits are only turning their backs on the living truth that would give them much happiness there and later here. To-day man is sufficiently developed to know the full truth which has always been known to the initiates since man began his life on earth, and when he learns the real value of this work that he is meant to do, he will wish that he had been more open-minded. To know that only his own stupidity and his desire for the material things of life on earth have stood between him and the wonderful advantages God meant for him, will be a great blow to his vanity.

To realize that he was given every opportunity over and over again and that he deliberately shut his eyes to the chances he was given, will be a revelation to him of his

LESSONS ON SYMPATHY

exceeding blindness. To know that day by day he turned his back on the great things of life for things of no real importance, will show him of how little worth and judgment he really is, and yet, in spite of the fact that he is of little value, all things great are designed for him and for his pleasure by his loving Father, and all that is asked in return is that he should follow his higher nature and willingly turn to the Father of all and try to do His will there on earth. When he begins to understand this and to work with his full strength, following the light that is shown, he will be of the Circles of Sympathy, and when he is once fully of these Circles, he will be alive to the great need of awakening all those who sleep.

Even if he only arrests their attention for a moment, the seed is sown, and even if they sink back into indifference and sleep, they have gone one step in the right direction, so no effort is lost which does not

LIFE IN THE CIRCLES

antagonize. Knowing the tremendous importance of this truth to every living soul, those who are of the Circles of Sympathy give their best effort to helping each one who needs help in any way. No one can tell the result of what he does, for when he gives material help he often opens the doors to further and spiritual help afterwards.

To always be on the watch for wise opportunities to sow that seed which will be of greatest benefit to those who struggle there on earth, is to be of the Circles of Sympathy.

This is the first lesson on Sympathy.
Love.

SECOND LESSON ON SYMPATHY

To be of those who are in the world with all their heart and with all their sympathy and yet are able to hold their own spiritual light, means work and study and learning self-control, for only in this way can one hold one's sympathy through frivolity, weakness and even degradation.

To look through the outside covering, whatever it may be, for the spark of the spirit, and to try to fan it into actual flame, and to feel that no human being no matter how apparently worthless, is to be allowed to die without an effort being made to arouse him to his real place in God's plan for each one to whom He has given life and power forever, is to be of these Circles.

Life and power are indestructible and can never be obliterated. They emanate directly from God and must be as He is

LIFE IN THE CIRCLES

eternal. But as in His wisdom God has given complete freedom to man to decide the use he chooses to make of his powers, so he can turn them from constructive to destructive forces. When man goes on the wrong path, he transforms the energy that has been given him into energy that can be used against the powers for good, and, as we have explained before in these teachings, all energy must come to the light, that is, come under God's spiritual laws as obedient forces, and here is the reason for the tremendous importance of man's life on earth.

If he refuses to learn the lesson for which he was made, the lesson of loving obedience to His Creator, he must return to earth again in order to try again to learn it. Each time he returns he will be of less value until he either achieves complete victory over his lower nature or until he has proved himself utterly worthless. Each time he returns his spiritual power is

LESSONS ON SYMPATHY

lessened and he belongs to less powerful forces, and he can only regain his power by supreme effort and tremendous self-sacrifice. Therefore it is most important to his future that man should not waste time in learning obedience or risk diminution of power by having to return again to learn that lesson. Those who are of the Circles of Sympathy will be alive to this danger for each one of their fellow-men, and will spare no effort to make them realize this penalty of lost time.

To be of these Circles we must keep very close to the hearts of all with whom we come in contact. No least antagonism must ever be allowed to enter and no time must be wasted in following the things of the lower nature that only antagonize, and all of life must be an effort to learn the lesson of understanding love.

To be of these Circles of Sympathy no petty animosity nor trivial hurt feeling may enter in. Nothing done to you by

LIFE IN THE CIRCLES

another must disturb your serenity of soul nor the love borne for that individual. Complete detachment from thought of self and complete understanding and sympathy with the frailties of those who have not yet this inner light, must be in your soul and mind at all times.

To do one's work daily in this spirit is to be fully in one's Circles.

This is the second lesson on Sympathy.
Love.

THIRD LESSON ON SYMPATHY

When man lives in close sympathy with all about him, and when he has so learned self-control that at all times and under all circumstances he can be master of himself and his moods, he will be of great power, and each day that he practises this control adds to his power. As he works among those who seek the light he will be able to give more and more fully of the truth he is learning, and each day's progress will teach him more of these spiritual laws.

Only through his wisdom and his apprehension of this spiritual light can he learn how to transform physical energy into spiritual power, and when through his hard and constant effort he has learned how to do this, he will begin to be of those Circles of healing and love which we call the Circles of Love.

LIFE IN THE CIRCLES

But before he can be really of full power he must learn how to be master of each one of the other and earlier Circles, and until he is complete master of Will, he cannot be fully of the Circle of Knowledge. This however does not prevent his knowledge of the work of these other Circles nor his participation in that work, and all the work that he does himself adds to his power to comprehend the full truth.

As his comprehension deepens his radiance grows and his power of understanding will become more acute, and as this spiritual power increases he will be more and more fully in the light. Physical power is acted on and often weakened by the light rays, but spiritual power is always strengthened by the light. To be of this power one must be consciously guided by spiritual guides. Only through their instruction can it grow in intensity, for only through their guidance can it be

LESSONS ON SYMPATHY

so wisely used that it is not dissipated by the use made of it.

All spiritual power is given for work in God's world, to be used in helping others and in showing the way to the light and love of God. It can only be wisely used in this work, for if otherwise used it becomes destructive force, and this is what the story of Satan tells.

To have been of the great spiritual powers and to have fallen from all power to be only of the destructive forces of the universe, knowing that ultimate defeat lies before them and therefore struggling with desperate energy to delay the inevitable end, is the story of all who ally themselves with evil powers, and Lucifer or Satan, who was the greatest of the angels, is truly the leader of these forces of darkness.

All the periods of spiritual development have been succeeded by waves of unbelief in the truth of the teachings, and one after another of the true stories, given by in-

LIFE IN THE CIRCLES

spiration to men, have been discarded as figments of their fancy. Man in the arrogance of his little knowledge really thinks he could have planned a better universe and pushes aside all evidence that does not suit his belief of the moment for the world as he conceives it, and so he has discarded many bits of truth which would be guides to him in his search for knowledge if he were not so blinded by material things. As his eyes open to the real truth he will go back and pick up many of these bits to make up his whole belief in the things that have been given by inspiration, and each day will add to his knowledge of God's exceeding wisdom which has been evidenced in the freedom He has given to man.

To have created a universe that was free from struggle would have been to have made puppets without character, for only by struggle and effort can character be built on earth, and to man is given the op-

LESSONS ON SYMPATHY

portunity to ally himself with powers that are limitless in their work for creation, but he must, in order to so ally himself, willingly turn to God, ready to obediently follow wherever the guides point the way, and only when he consciously works with his guides can he be sure of that way. Then he can make no mistake in his path through following his own inclination or what others desire for him.

Yet these guides, though they are always ready to help when man's heart is open to them, will not interfere with his daily life and struggle, because that experience is for his development, and through this daily and hourly struggle his power will grow. But as he turns to God in prayer, strength and wisdom are given him and more and more light comes into his life, and this light leads him into the path of that peace which passeth understanding.

This is the third lesson on Sympathy. Love.

FOURTH LESSON ON SYMPATHY

All truth that the wisest and most learned of men can acquire on earth is only the beginning of knowledge. Life goes on for all eternity and all of life is a development of power of mind and heart and spirit.

Just as the alphabet is the beginning of learning to read, so the beginning of spiritual power is shown in the willingness to turn to God and follow what He wills, and this can only be done by each one for himself and constitutes man's free gift of himself to His Father. As long as he thus freely gives himself his spirit grows and all possibilities lie open before him, and this open door to all power can never be closed except by his own desire. Only when his spirit becomes arrogant and no longer obedient will he lose his guides, and

LESSONS ON SYMPATHY

there is never any time when he cannot turn again of his own will to God. But as this knowledge grows, the knowledge of the importance of his work grows too, and the effect of disobedience will be more clearly seen. Therefore his punishment for that disobedience will be the greater.

To deliberately choose to be of the evil powers who can never know real happiness is hardly conceivable, yet this may happen to one whose foundation is not built on humbleness of spirit and a real obedience. Therefore to purge one's heart and spirit of all arrogance is one of the first steps to complete success. No elation over the power gained must be allowed one's self, only happiness in the privilege of being allowed to do this work.

To keep this attitude of mind in all times and under all conditions whether of good or evil appearance, judged from the standpoint of those who judge with earthly judgment, takes self-control. To feel no

LIFE IN THE CIRCLES

whit superior to those who have not this light from lack of opportunity or from other reasons, will take all that one has of self-control and modesty of spirit. Each time a feeling of elation at one's own light enters, one's light is dimmed. Only the elation that comes from having helped another can be allowed, and that is rather the happiness of being privileged to do this work.

To so work that day after day one can point to one helped there and another here, while each day brings new understanding of spiritual laws, is to be of the Circles of Sympathy, and as sympathy grows and love develops more and more, one's spirit becomes that of a little child who knows that all good comes to him from the father who loves and guards him, for until the flower of divine love blossoms in the heart which has become as the heart of a happy, loving little child, one cannot fully enter into the Kingdom of Heaven.

LESSONS ON SYMPATHY

Utter selflessness, entire sympathy, perfect love is the sum of human perfection to which we must aspire, and only when we have started on this path do we begin to come into our rightful inheritance. Then our sympathy goes out to all in the world, no matter what or where, and in the expression of that sympathy we take our full place in these Circles. When no one is too degraded and no one too lowly to enter into our hearts, then we are of the Circles of Sympathy.

This is the fourth lesson on Sympathy. Love.

FIFTH LESSON ON SYMPATHY

When man turns with his whole heart and mind to doing God's work in the world, he will find new avenues of activity on every side. Everywhere he can learn new spiritual truths for which before he had no vision and everywhere he will find those who need help to start on the way while they are yet in the world.

To be responsible for the failure of another to do his part because you failed to give him that light which you hold for him, is a great responsibility. When you see the mistakes and failures which are due to your negligence, you will be appalled at the many opportunities which you have failed to seize. Not that your mistakes can make the lives of others not worth while, but that your mistakes may delay them there on earth since you are the guardian of

LESSONS ON SYMPATHY

God's light for those with whom you come in contact. When you fail to share and diffuse that light you fail not only in your duty to God but also in your duty to your brother and, most of all, to yourself, for sympathy would always share and help and when sympathy does not enter in there must be selfishness, and selfishness is a deadly sin.

There is no such thing as a vacuum in nature and the way to get rid of evil is to cultivate good, for two forces cannot occupy the same space at the same time.

Those of the Circles of Sympathy are always watching for the chance to help and are never blind to suffering. As their light grows their understanding of humanity grows, and the intuition by which they read men's hearts develops, and they are able to see things to which others are utterly blind.

Only to those whose spiritual under-

LIFE IN THE CIRCLES

standing is of a high order will the light be given, and through this ability to read men's hearts they will be able to help as they could in no wise do without this power, and only when they have this power are they fully in the Circles of Sympathy, and only when all selfishness is eradicated from their hearts can they have this power to its full extent.

To gain complete control of their will they must carefully watch each word and every thought, and only in this way can they reach to spiritual heights in strength of purpose. Yet the reward is so far beyond man's conception that there is no compensation for its loss. Each victory gained over self brings more strength for the next step and firmer purpose, while each failure brings weakened will.

Every day, every hour, every minute counts, and the great victory is to the steadfast of purpose. Carry your light on

LESSONS ON SYMPATHY

high and work steadily, praying constantly, and fail not!

This is the fifth lesson on Sympathy. Love.

SIXTH LESSON ON SYMPATHY

To fail to work while on earth is to fail to be of one's Circles and that is to fail to be of full power on earth and after. As lost time is never completely made up, so lost opportunity brings the sad punishment of lessened spiritual power and of a lower degree in the Circles to which one belongs. Only when one fully grasps one's inner light and works to the best of one's ability there on earth can he continue in the Circles to which he was born.

As his spirit is a spark of God's spirit and as his body is a product of his father and his mother, so his soul is the result of the fusion of their moral qualities, but though these qualities may place him high in the Circles, he can only maintain that place by his own effort.

Study, work, steadfast purpose, and liv-

LESSONS ON SYMPATHY

ing the life on earth that can be lived according to God's laws, are necessary to keep his place, and only when he does this will he fully enter into the Circles which are his heritage. To each one is given this opportunity time after time, though many are not aware of the significance of their choice, but the choice is always given over and over again, and the door of spiritual life stands open for all who will even peep therein.

To realize this and to work to the limit of one's strength that others may reap the benefit of one's work is to be of the Circles of Sympathy. To desire the spiritual life for everyone around us that they may enter into their full heritage, is to be of the Circles of Sympathy. To leave no stone unturned that will waken them to the great meaning of life, and no sacrifice of time or strength unmade which will help them, is to be of the Circles of Sympathy, and when one is fully of these Circles,

LIFE IN THE CIRCLES

one's heart is filled with the great love of all mankind that carries one into the Circles of Love.

This is the sixth lesson on Sympathy. Love.

CHAPTER VII

LESSONS ON LOVE

FIRST LESSON ON LOVE

To enter these last and greatest Circles is to be of really unlimited power, for before one is fully in these Circles he must be a master of all the others and of entire self-control, filled with love for all mankind and completely detached from all materialism and from all selfishness. Only when the soul has attained to the greatest heights of earthly love and self-denial can it walk in the light of these Circles, and to that soul nothing is impossible.

All of the life of the spirit is open to it and all the light of knowledge and under-

LIFE IN THE CIRCLES

standing. Not many achieve to this degree but those who do are utterly happy, because to them is revealed the eternal truth and they know and have faith in the ultimate end. To them the dark places are filled with light and to them the little shadows are full of benefit as gentle discipline.

To these happy souls the change from earthly to spiritual life is but a step and a joyous freedom from the heavy weight of materialism. As a child goes happily through school, they go happily through the school of earthly life. Each day's work well done is one step further on the way and each step brings clearer understanding.

To walk through life gently, filled with love and kindness, bearing a lighted torch for all to see and for all to light theirs by, is a well-lived life, and, simple as it seems, there are few who so live. Yet this is the life lived by Christ and the example we are

LESSONS ON LOVE

told to follow, and this is the life of the Kingdom.

To have a few much-loved friends, to live simply with an open heart to all who seek light, and to be always ready to help each one who asks for help, is to live the life of the spirit.

To be gentle, to be kind to all, to be a living example of the faith you try to live by, will take you far into the Circles of Love.

This is the first lesson on Love. Love.

SECOND LESSON ON LOVE

The supreme height of love that can be reached on earth was attained by Christ and, through His knowledge of spiritual laws, He worked the miracles that to-day science is trying to ignore or explain away. These miracles were all done according to laws, for God does not break His laws, but spiritual laws transcend physical laws and can in this way work what the unknowing call miracles, and this has been done at all times and in all ages since man has inhabited the earth.

There have always been those initiates who knew and could work with these laws, and in this way much knowledge has been handed down from one to another. When the ages have given up their secrets it will be found that the light of spiritual knowledge has always been aglow for those who

LESSONS ON LOVE

sought to find, and that no one has truly sought in vain. Always this light is given in some way or another if he who seeks is in earnest and has a humble and obedient spirit.

Little by little his knowledge and understanding will grow until his whole idea of life will change, and a new and constructive plan will take the place of what seemed to him a meaningless jumble, and as his ideas change his life itself must change also and conform to those laws which he begins to dimly apprehend.

Not that he should change his mode of life or his place therein or his friends, but that now, with this light in his spirit, he can give more fully that sympathy and love which bring him into close relationship with all who are near him. As the range of his sympathy enlarges the circle of his influence is increased, and as he sheds his light he illumines all about him, and so his work is done.

LIFE IN THE CIRCLES

To work in this way day after day is to be of those powers who work for God. It is living up to the highest possibilities one can and it is preparing one's self for further development, for all of life is a constant development if one obeys those laws to which he is subject. All do not work consciously in the right direction but all do not achieve success, and those who do work consciously are laying foundations that will surprise them when they become aware of the importance of life there and here, and the greatest of all foundation stones is love.

All spiritual life is founded thereon and all development must come through love. Without love there can be no spiritual life and without love there can be no real progress. Only as one cultivates and develops this spiritual quality can one really grow, and the more perfect the love the more completely one is free from selfishness. Filled with love, the spirit blossoms like a

LESSONS ON LOVE

lovely flower full of perfume and giving delight to all who come near. Without love, it lives and dies and no one cares or is the poorer for its passing.

Love is like a ray of sunshine which warms and cheers each one whom it touches. Love is like a magical wand which can transmute all baser metals into the pure gold of spirit. Love can never be bought or sold. Love is of all emotions the most divine and the most perfect expression of God.

This is the second lesson on Love. Love.

THIRD LESSON ON LOVE

As man begins to develop as he is intended to develop on earth, he expresses more and more perfectly the divine attributes. Being made in the image of God, he will be expected to attain to his full stature as he develops under His laws, and until he comes into full perfection he will not be fully developed.

Christ came as an example of what can be achieved on earth if one will work with one's spiritual guides. But development does not end with earth life nor can perfection be attained there. Even we who have gone many steps beyond you have no conception of the ultimate end, but as we see the wonderful development of our teachers, we have some idea of where we are going, and as our ideals rise our

LESSONS ON LOVE

struggles to attain become more steadfast and persistent.

Once the foundations are securely laid the work grows in importance and in joy and sympathy. But even here our struggles are by no means over. The road to perfection is a long hard struggle, but our life can be filled with joy by following our guides instead of trying to fight on in the darkness alone, and he who works with joy will accomplish far more for himself and all about him than he who strives no matter how hard, with a stern and set face.

To be joyous, to be gay, to be loving and without thought of self brings a great reward. To lighten the gloomy places and to pour love and sunshine into the dark spots is to do one's duty fully. As the difference between a bright and sunshiny day and a dark and gloomy one, so is the difference between a joyous and a sad spirit.

To walk erect in God's sunshine with joy and love filling one's heart and soul is to

LIFE IN THE CIRCLES

be of the Circles of Love, but the foundation stones of these Circles must be laid in the Circles of Will, where perfect self-control brings serenity of spirit which no materialism can disturb.

Strive, study, work and love to the utmost of your ability, and be of these radiant Circles who wait eagerly for you.

This is the third lesson on Love. Love.

FOURTH LESSON ON LOVE

As one lifts one's spirit towards the things of the spirit which alone give life to all material things, one comes into a new relationship with life. Gradually a new apprehension of the spiritual meaning will fill one's life and soul, and constructive action allying one's self to one's spiritual guides will take the place of the old purposeless life.

When we realize that every action has a spiritual and deep significance, if we live as we should, we will carefully guard that action and see that it has the right significance for others and for ourselves. To hold with perfect serenity a thought of perfect love in all our relationships and contacts, is to live under the law of Love.

To be undisturbed by the actions of others, knowing that all unkindness is only

LIFE IN THE CIRCLES

a lack of light and that every broken law brings its own punishment to the sinner, is to live under the law of love. To know that the reason one is in the world is for development through loving, unselfish aid to those who have lost or who cannot find their way, is to work in one's Circles.

To give the best that is in one freely and lovingly at all times is to be of the Circles of Love. To purge one's heart of all malice and of all desire to hurt again those who have hurt us, is to be of the Circles of Love which lead further into eternal life than any dream who have not passed the portals to life here.

To live knowing that what you call death is the open door to all real life and opportunity, and that those who have come here would no more willingly return than a child would return to the embryo life, is to begin to realize the significance of life.

To live in the light of the Circles of Love is to realize that we live tenderly guarded

LESSONS ON LOVE

and guided by a loving, all-wise power, and to cast all fear aside and trust to that power, following where the guides lead and helping all who are near. And to him who struggles upward on the path will be given a full and complete freedom from earthly fears and from material, destructive forces, and to him will come the perfect and utter serenity of peace which those of the world can never otherwise find.

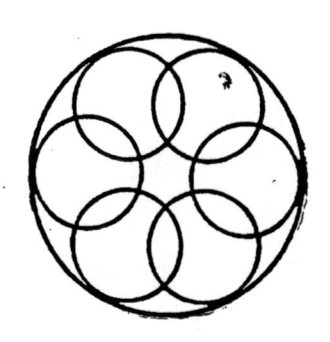

This is the fourth lesson on Love. Love.

FIFTH LESSON ON LOVE

To live in the light of God's love is to live in tender, loving sympathy with all who are near us. Only when His love is shared with all with whom we come in contact can we be said to really possess it ourselves, and no living thing and no human being, no matter how seemingly unworthy, is ever outside this love, and in order to fulfill our function in life, we must fully express this love and tender thought for all who are near us.

As God guards and guides us day by day, leaving us perfectly free to do what we will, so should we do to those around us, and no departure from the path pointed out by us in life must ever influence our thought of love for the wilful one. As we fail with greater understanding, we must expect others to fail. Are we to receive

LESSONS ON LOVE

forgiveness and not forgive others? And the quantity of our mercy will show the quality of our loving understanding.

Only when we put in practice the love we know and desire can we come into fuller understanding of that love, and as we consciously day by day and hour by hour, practise the attributes of love, we begin to realize what love can be. Yet the highest expression of love on earth is a poor shadow of real love, and as we develop we learn little by little of God's love for us, but we can only learn this through the expression of love for others. We must express love in order to acquire more power of loving, and the fuller the expression the greater the power.

To be of these Circles is to be of limitless power, but to be of these Circles is to be of utter and loving perfection. Few achieve on earth but those who really try are on the way and will achieve one day, and while everyone must eventually come

LIFE IN THE CIRCLES

under the law, only those who begin during their life there come into full power.

To be of full power means not to have failed to turn while there to God and to have consciously sought for guidance, and it also means to live the life to the best of one's ability, doing all that one can for others and, while in the world and of the world, keeping one's spiritual point of view. Only complete harmony and serenity can accomplish this and only by daily and hourly effort can this serenity be found.

To be entirely detached from all material things and to be of the spiritual life only in heart, while outwardly living as all others, is to be of the Circles. To rise above all earthly troubles into the pure ether of spiritual life and power, gaily meeting the daily disturbances of earthly life and filled with the joy of helpfulness, is to be of the Circles of Love.

To express in all relationships the tender

LESSONS ON LOVE

sympathy of loving understanding, to do all that is humanly possible to smooth the path for others, to turn minute by minute to the loving, all-wise Father who holds all His children tenderly in the hollow of His hand, knowing that while living in this trust only good can possibly reach you, is to be of the Circles of Love.

This is the fifth lesson on Love. Love.

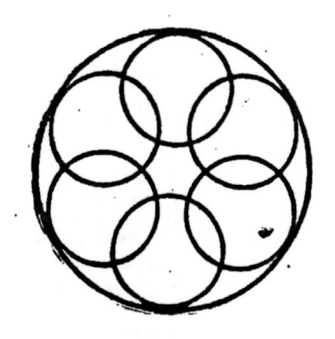

SIXTH LESSON ON LOVE

The fullest development that can come on earth leads one into these Circles of Love, and only when one's lesson is perfectly learned is one of these highest Circles of all.

Before we can be of these Circles we must be perfect in all others, and to few will come the complete mastery essential, but one day's work may take one so very far into the Circles that one can never tell how far he may go. One great act of unselfish love may carry one to supreme spiritual heights, just as one careless, selfish act may cast one very far down in the scale, but the oftener one rises to the heights the easier it becomes to remain there.

As it is difficult to acquire complete self-control, so it is difficult to become a really spiritual being, for man is not born a

LESSONS ON LOVE

spirit and he can only become one through his will and his effort. To be of the highest needs supreme effort and a great desire that never falters. Yet all may achieve if they will without ceasing and if they steadfastly lead the life of the spirit.

To be of those who achieve will be to be of those shining ones whose work will be pronounced good by the Lord who judges, and to these will come a reward that is only for them to know when their work is finally judged.

But as they work, to them is given a peace that passeth understanding and a joy that never fails.

This is the sixth lesson on Love. Love.

APPENDIX

(A number of questions and answers received after the lessons and having no particular bearing on the teaching, but which we have added as being of interest.)

(What is the most important thing to teach men?)
"Love, and a willingness to help others."
"Whenever you work constructively for others with no thought of self, you work for the spiritual forces."

"'Circles' are forces for the best teaching of mankind, and if you work with 'Circles' you will help many who would otherwise be without help on earth."

(Must I think of —— as better off because he died?)
"No, think of him as alive."

(When will we be able to write [automatically] alone?)
"That depends on your willingness to obliterate your own desire."

(Can we ask for those we want to reach and get messages from them?)
"No, not now."
(Will we be able to later?)
"Able when you learn the laws better and know how

APPENDIX

and for whom to ask. No one is allowed to seek them for curiosity."

(Would communication with the next world be the best thing that could come to men now?)
"Yes, it would end all fear and be the best of work, and if we knew, it would bring peace for all."

"All work that is for the world is for God. 'Love your brother as yourself' is the command of Christ, and all who would follow Him must follow this truth."
(But when people show hostility towards us how can we love them?)
"Look only at their good qualities, and do not let what they do to you influence."

(When a person in our world dies, who meets them in the next world?)
"They will be met by those whom they knew and loved on earth, and also by helpful ones."
(When next I see —— will it be the same between us?)
"Yes, you will see no change at first, and then you will see much growth and beauty."

"We will leave you until you believe—until you work well for others. This is only for you if you profit by it spiritually."
(This was written one day in the beginning of our work when we spoke to each other of the desire we felt to get everyone out of the way so that we could be

APPENDIX

free to work. After the above sentence was written we tried for nearly half an hour but we could not get one word more that day. And the next day the first words were, "Are we better today? Are we more loving?"

(Do those in the next world do what they are told to do or do they choose their work?)

"There is a choice and each one does what he wants to do."

(Spirit, am I to be entirely guided by you in life?)

"No, you must be independent and go on your own way as you will, but if you take the right way we will help you. If you take the other way the guides wait."

(I have been so lonely today. Has that interfered with my work?)

"When you shut the door of your heart, we too are shut out from you. It will soon pass. All progress is in waves and you will go on again."

"We must cast out fear. God is love and you are His child."

(Do people in the other world feel like that all the time?)

"There are all kinds of spirits here too, and only those who are awake feel as they should and as they must. As a man dies in the world so he is born here, and he must work much harder because he has wasted much time."

"We are able to reach you only through your attention being voluntarily given to us."

APPENDIX

"Children have a special world of their own and you cannot always reach them. Children grow faster and better in a place where there are no deterrent spirits."

(Personal communication from ——.)

"Tell G— that the little children (who had died some months before) are well and happy and that we are together very often."

(H. You know that G— is here?)

"Yes, I wrote for her."

(H. A little while ago you told us that you never saw the children, how is it that you are with them now?)

"I am beginning to know how to reach them."

(H. Who cares for them?)

"Loving spirits who want to serve children."

(H. When you see them is it as it was on earth?)

"Yes, but you have much greater love,—and will to reach them is needed."

(How should one try to put one's self in communication with the spiritual world?)

"Work for those in the world and pray for guidance."

(Spirit, when you say "pray" what do you mean?)

"The lifting up of your heart and soul to God. The bodily position is of no consequence,—the attitude of the mind is the thing that counts."

(In order to be safe from interference in trying automatic writing the attitude of mind steadily held is most

APPENDIX

important, and until one has learned how to do this, one should not really try to write.)

"There are interfering forces who wish to prevent lessons being given to God's children, and they will interfere whenever you are not strong of purpose and pure of heart."

One must hold "a clear vision of assured expectation of the truth and an attitude of prayer. No outside force can reach you if you have the right attitude."

(Spirit, is there any way to give proof to those who search?)

"No, each one must search for himself, and the door will be opened to each who seeks."

"All who help their brothers are living the life. Those who are unselfish are able to find their guides very quickly, and only when man is in touch with his guides can he reach those who have gone before. All who have lost are anxious to reach their loved ones and only through these guides can they do so."

"Love is never wasted on man or beast. All that the world can give cannot buy love. All that money can do cannot buy love. All that man dares or tries cannot buy love. All that the greatest can bestow cannot buy love. Love is a free gift of the soul that must be given, not bought, and love is worth more than all else in the world. Love is the highest expression of life, and love is all-including, all-enduring, all-embracing."

APPENDIX

(Message received as we were going away for some weeks in September, 1919, "Is there anything to say now that we are leaving?")

"All that you do or say must be in love. All that you do or say must be in wisdom. All that you do or say must be in every way after the highest that you know. All that you think must be sweet and pure. All that you dream must be of how to do God's will. All that you dream will come true. All that you dream by night and day is for your best effort. All that can be done to keep you in the right path will be done."

"For when the light fails on earth those who have worked with the Circles will be greatly rewarded, and the time is short for all on earth."

"Love to the full of each one's capacity all who are on earth and here."

"Love to the uttermost those who are near you."

"Love to the outside limits those who offend you."

"Pray to God for clear vision and belief."

November 17th, 1919.

(During the writing of the lessons on Will.)

(We had both gone through a very trying day during which we had been annoyed, upset and cross, and when we started our work the writing began:)

"We are here and you really should do better."

(Which of us should do better?)

"Both. For awhile you are intended to work together, both having the same tendency to lack of self-

APPENDIX

control, and both being of the same Circles; and we must control ourselves if we are to work well."

November 26th, 1919.

"We are here and we are willing to tell you all that you can understand but you must study more."

(You mean study the lessons?)

"Yes, and everything that tells you what the work of life is."

December 8th, 1919.

(One of the sentences being long and not clearly written we had great difficulty in reading it. Finally A. asked "Will you give us the first part of that sentence again?")

"Work.'

(After some further attempts on our part.)

"Are we to work or play?"

(A little later after more futile attempts and when we were discouraged.)

"Are we to do what you wish only?"

(In the midst of a sentence in the fifth lesson on will.)

"We will not continue."

(Oh, may we not finish the lesson?)

"—— is not concentrating."

(I know, but I will try.)

"We will try again."

APPENDIX

December 9th, 1919.

(During the lessons on Knowledge.)
(In the midst of a sentence.)
"We will continue tomorrow."
(. . . Oh, my mind was wandering! Was it that? I am so sorry.)
"You must learn to concentrate. Are we to do whatever you wish or will you do as we ask? We will teach you great things only if you use them wisely. We are satisfied with your intentions but you must work harder. Study more, love more, teach more. Are you satisfied with us? Love."

December 15th, 1919.

"We are here and we will only be able to work for a short time today."
(Nothing wrong with us is there?)
"No, we are very busy."
(A little later.)
"We will continue tomorrow and we will take up the question of transmigration of souls." (See the first lesson on Knowledge, sentence beginning "Spirit has existed always, etc.")

December 26th, 1919.

(Spirit, —— wanted me to ask if the teaching in the Old Testament was received in writing like this?)
"No, by personal inspiration."
(They received it through their minds?)

APPENDIX

"Yes——"

(Have all great teachers received their teaching from intercourse with your world?)

"Yes, but some prophets and teachers have had much more in their own souls than others."

(A. to H. Do you suppose that light and radium and the love of God are all terms for the same thing?)

"You are beginning to apprehend."

(After the first lesson on Joy.)

(Spirit, is there any virtue in fasting?)

"All spiritual teachers have worked with fasting and with prayer."

(Should we give up meat or keep to any diet? I mean would it advance us in spiritual power?)

"To be of the inner life will require giving up grosser material things and meat is a strong material food."

December 30th, 1919.

(Should we fast? And to what extent?)

"If you can do so without hurting yourself it would lessen the material hold."

December 31st, 1919.

(During the third lesson on Joy.)

(Before the writing began we were discussing a friend who would not admit the possibility of a future life.)

"We are here and we will tell you what to say to those who do not believe in the continuity of personal identity. Even when the world is not understanding

APPENDIX

this eventually will be clear, because the whole scientific world believes in the indestructibility of matter and energy, and life is a form of energy and cannot be destroyed. Even when a drop of water is absorbed in a cloud it will still be a drop of water; and so it will be with man. He will retain all the personality that he has ever had, and even his outward form will be recognizable."

January 4th, 1920.

(Spirit, may I ask a question?)
"Ask."
(What line of study should we follow? I know the vague reading I do is not enough.)
"Read all that the prophets and teachers have written from time to time and your guides will tell you what is eternally true and what is only man's imagination."
(We don't work nearly as hard as we should, do we?)
"No, but you will learn."

January 2nd, 1920.

(After a day's work in which we had not been attentive.)
"If you are to continue this work you must try to work better and learn to prayerfully concentrate on what we are teaching. You will not be able to work if you do not live the life. Are we to be willing to work always when you wish, and you as you choose?

APPENDIX

We are always at your call and you are not willing to work daily. Are we to be put aside for worldly interests? God is waiting while you play."

January 3rd, 1920.

(The work today began,)
"Are we really ready to work now?"
"Are we pure in heart?"? "Are we willing to be of God's obedient children?"
"Are we to do as He wishes?"
"God is willing that you should have all earthly pleasures if you put them in their proper place."

January 5th, 1920.

"Those who have gone to higher spheres can always return, but those in the lower spheres cannot come into the higher places until they have earned the right."
(May I ask a question?)
"Ask."
(Is the reason that we have been able to get one or two messages lately because we are getting a little more into these Circles?)
"We are never willing to tell where a student stands."

January 7th, 1920.

(In reference to a proposed trip that would postpone our lessons.)
"We are always willing to have you work first for others, and then for this teaching for yourselves."

APPENDIX

January 13th, 1920.

"We are here and we are ready. When all that we can do to teach is done we will stop working with you."

(But Spirit, you said you would work with us as long as we worked well. Is that so?)

"Yes, only if you do not do better we will wait."

(Are we failing to get the concentration that you expected?)

"Are we never to make you understand that you must work? When all these lessons have been finished and revised we will wait for you to be of further power before continuing. It will depend on yourselves entirely how soon we come back."

(If we work hard will it be necessary for you to go?)

"No, that depends on you and when you are willing to be of utter and complete obedience."

(My spirit is willing but habit is strong.)

"Habit is to be broken. All do not believe what they are told, but you know. All do not believe what they hear, but you both are well informed. And to be given everything and not use it well is to be willing to be of the evil forces."

(Have you anything to say to P— [a visitor]?)

"She has the necessary power but she must work and live the life in order to develop it without interference. To live the life, one must study and learn utter obedience to all that God wills, and eradicate wilfulness."

"She should try to write only when she knows how

APPENDIX

to hold the necessary attitude of mind to prevent her being used by outside powers."

(Have you any objection to my going to a medium who seems to be an honest person?)

"We do not like it for we want you to develop your own power."

January 21st, 1920.

(Here follows an extraordinary experience. Some months before this A. had entrusted a friend with a very delicate confidential mission in the execution of which she felt he had not understood the confidence she had placed in him, and had failed in a matter of the utmost importance to her. In discussing this one day with H. she voiced this opinion, and H.'s advice was that a letter should be written by A. to Mr. Blank telling him frankly the feeling that A. had and so clearing the way for possible explanations that might lead to a better understanding; for to live the life as we were told we must it would not allow harboring any feeling of bitterness.

That night the letter was written but it was unconsciously phrased in a spirit of extreme bitterness, and when received was a great shock to Mr. Blank who was unconscious of any wrong-doing, and who felt that it was unjust and entirely misrepresented his actions. This at the time was unknown to H. who did not know that letter had been sent.

The next three days' experience follows.)

APPENDIX

"We are here and we are going to give you a lesson that is for you alone.

"Whenever anyone has anything against his brother he must wait until he can tell him without anger or bitterness and he must close his heart to all temper or feeling of bitterness. This he can only do through a strong determination and much prayer. To harbor any feeling of unkindness prevents all work of this kind. Our guides can only reach us when our hearts are those of loving, little children, free from all uncharitableness. And until we obey the command of Christ to be at one with all whom we know, we are outside the reach of all of our Circles."

(A. I don't know what command they refer to.)

"We will not continue until you are in a different mood."

(A. I am not conscious of not being in the right mood.)

(Then followed a discussion over the text and we asked if it was, "Therefore if thou bring thy gift to the altar, and there rememberest that thy brother hath ought against thee; Leave there thy gift before the altar, and go thy way; first be reconciled to thy brother, and then come and offer thy gift." (Math. 5:23. 24.)

"That is a command to be in love and sympathy with all whom you know. Think this over carefully and pray for guidance while you are away from each other." (H. was leaving town for some days.) "We will be near you and we will help you but until all trace of

APPENDIX

uncharitableness has been purged from your hearts we will wait to continue the lessons."

"Work hard, learn sympathy and tenderness toward all whom you know and be a loving child of God, showing only kindness toward every living thing, or lose your Circles until you do as they require."

(H. That sounds like an alternative.)

"It is an alternative, if you do not love with all your force there on earth and cherish anger toward anyone or thing."

January 27th, 1920.

(H. was absent several days during which time A. had written Mr. Blank a letter of explanation and apology, and felt that all that could be done had been done.)

"We are here and we are not satisfied that you are working to the best of your ability."

(H. Could you tell us why you are not satisfied?)

"We are not able to see the light in your inner lives that should be there."

(H. I know just what you mean but we do try.)

"We will wait until you are really ready to go on."

"Are you pure of heart? Are you pure of mind?"

"Are you being loving to all of your fellows?"

"Are you sorry when you hurt another and are you willing to make amends to the uttermost?"

"Have you written to say that you are very sorry?"

"Has every trace of bitterness been obliterated from your heart?"

APPENDIX

"Pray more and tomorrow we will work."

(H. Won't you give us a lesson today?)

"Not until your light is clearer. We will be with you today in all your work and prayers."

(Here we had a talk on the occasion of this discipline, A. saying that she had written an apology and did not see what else she could do.)

"But you hurt a fellow-man, and when the remembrance of the hurt feeling is entirely wiped out by your actions your power will be again what it was."

"Work and pray. Love."

January 28th, 1920.

"We are here and we are not yet satisfied. We will tell you what must be done.'

"Are you in close sympathy with all around you?"

"Are you very tender and loving to all who worry over outside things? Are you close to God?"

"Are you in close touch with all men who come to you?"

"Work hard and pray for more light and guidance. Tomorrow we will try again."

(H. How are we to know what to do?)

"We will tell you when you are in the right path again."

(A. to H. Apparently as long as anyone feels grieved at us for something for which we are responsible, we ourselves lose in spiritual power.)

"Are you sure of what you think?"

APPENDIX

"Are you in the love of all others?"

"Are you in a world of material desire to be weak or to grow?"

"Are we willing to write whenever you will and you shirk the work that develops your power? Are you sure of your own desire for advancement?"

"Love."

January 29th, 1920.

"We are here and we can work today. Whenever you are in doubt of anything we are waiting to help you."

"Love and work and study and slowly grow into a fuller comprehension of spiritual things." (Then began the first lesson on Understanding.)

February 3rd, 1920.

(One of us had been very unhappy over an attack made on one she dearly loved.)

"We are here and we are ready. Are we pure in heart and mind?"

"Are we purged of base thoughts?"

"Are we to be about God's work only, and are we willingly to forgive our enemies?"

"Are we to be of those who know what love can be, and will not practice it on earth whenever the irritation of outside trouble comes?"

(But to defend those one loves must be a part of love.)

APPENDIX

"Love is always to be defended but without anger or bitterness."

February 10th, 1920.

(H. Will you give me a word about Brady's death. A man who had died at the military hospital.)

"Can you doubt that all is well with him and that he is happier than he ever dreamed of being?"

February 13th, 1920.

"Sadness must be utterly and entirely shut out if one is to be of power. Those who allow themselves to be sad will not be able to do this work."

(Do you mean that it is an absolute duty to be cheerful?)

"It is God's law that His obedient children should be happy. All who work well will be cheerful and happy. Those who work well will be filled with a radiant content that is utter happiness."

February 14th, 1920.

"We will guide you at all times and our love is around you always" (here H. said, "This sounds like another control"), "but we will not be satisfied with weakness or poor work." (As the sentence was finished she added, "Oh no, this is *you* all right" and we both laughed.)

"We are happy when you laugh at our chiding and

APPENDIX

we are pleased with your understanding, but you must carry it into your living consciousness."

February 15th, 1920.

"We are not entirely satisfied but your efforts are being sustained by all the help that we can give you while you fail to utterly open the doors to us. We can only reach you when you pray and this must be your constant and unremitting attitude of mind. Work harder, dear children of earth! We need you and can only fully use you when you are more perfectly developed."

February 26th, 1920.

(I want to ask if this material life is just a delusion of the senses and if we will wake up from it as from a dream?)

"It is real and of the most serious importance to each one of you. The fight to dominate the material by the spiritual is no dream."

February 27th, 1920.

(Spirit, A.P. would like to know why material-minded people, such as ——, often get such spiritual communications?)

"We do not know how she is able to judge who is spiritual and who is material. Here we see the inner radiance, there you cannot see it."

(Does the degree of spiritual advancement of the

APPENDIX

one who receives the message have anything to do with the nature of the message received?)

"Not always. There are some human instruments who can transmit any message without in the least apprehending the meaning, but usually the one receiving must have spiritual apprehension or the message is distorted."

(Is an emanation of some physical matter necessary in all physical phenomena—such as this writing?)

"We use your physical force in conjunction with your psychic mind."

(Would there be more physical force if we were in a dark room?)

"All physical and material forces are of darkness, but spiritual power may be the same force regenerated through spiritual light and life."

(Would actual physical light mean increased spiritual perception?)

"No spiritual light can be increased by any lesser light. Only work and love can increase spiritual perception."

April 5th, 1920.

(At the end of the sixth lesson on Sympathy after A. had been ill and unable to write for some weeks.)

"Anne must rest and continue now to work."

"Love and joy to work with you again. Love and peace of mind to you, guarded as you are by your guides and loved ones."

(A. Was there anything that I could have done to have avoided this illness?)

APPENDIX

"You are paying the penalty of broken physical laws. One cannot overdo without breaking the law, and all broken laws either physical, moral or spiritual, bring their inevitable punishment."

April 14th, 1920.

"We are here and we are not able to write until you are a little more rested. When A. is a little stronger we will continue. We are not able to use you when you are so tired. We will be ready to work with you in two or three days now. Love, dear children."

May 4th, 1920.

"Do not continue. Anne is too tired." (We were correcting a lesson.)

(Anne said that she was not conscious of being tired and H. said she was surprised as she thought Anne was less tired than yesterday.)

"We are not sure of what you read." (This was during the reading of the lessons for revision.)

(Anne. Oh, now I understand. I did not know what you meant.)

"Good. We are satisfied. When you work well we get each word. Today we get very little and when you are concentrated we get it all."

APPENDIX

"You are paying the penalty of broken physical laws. One cannot overdo without breaking the law, and all broken laws either physical, moral or spiritual, bring their inevitable punishment."

April 14th, 1920.

"We are here and we are not able to write until you are a little more rested. When A. is a little stronger we will continue. We are not able to use you when you are so tired. We will be ready to work with you in two or three days now. Love, dear children."

May 4th, 1920.

"Do not continue. Anne is too tired." (We were correcting a lesson.)

(Anne said that she was not conscious of being tired and H. said she was surprised as she thought Anne was less tired than yesterday.)

"We are not sure of what you read." (This was during the reading of the lessons for revision.)

(Anne. Oh, now I understand. I did not know what you meant.)

"Good. We are satisfied. When you work well we get each word. Today we get very little and when you are concentrated we get it all."

Deacidified using the Bookkeeper process
Neutralizing agent Magnesium Oxide
Treatment Date Nov 2004

PreservationTechnologies
A WORLD LEADER IN PAPER PRESERVATION

111 Thomson Park Drive
Cranberry Township, PA 16066
(724) 779-2111